Dressed to Kill

Awakening the Warrior Princess

Emily Quintero-Spongberg

Be Blessed!
Emily Quintero-Spongberg

"A thief is only there to steal and kill and destroy. I came so they can have real and eternal life, more and better life than they ever dreamed of." (John 10:10 The Message)

A Positive Image Ministries

Glastonbury, CT

(860-781-2107)

Visit us at: www.apositiveimage.com

Dressed to Kill

Awakening the Warrior Princess

A study on Spiritual Warfare
and the Armor of God

Emily Quintero-Spongberg

Unless otherwise stated, all Scripture quotes are taken from the New International Version®, NIV®. Copyright © 1973, 1978, 1984, 2011 by Biblica, Inc.™ Used by permission of Zondervan. All rights reserved worldwide.

Other Scriptures are taken (as marked)

Scripture quotations marked (NLT) are taken from the Holy Bible, New Living Translation, copyright ©1996, 2004, 2015 by Tyndale House Foundation. Used by permission of Tyndale House Publishers, Carol Stream, Illinois 60188. All rights reserved.

Scripture quotations marked (MSG) are taken from THE MESSAGE, copyright © 1993, 2002, 2018 by Eugene H. Peterson. Used by permission of NavPress, represented by Tyndale House Publishers. All rights reserved.

Scripture quotations marked (KJV) are from The Authorized (King James) Version.

Copyright © 2021 Emily Quinter-Spongberg.

All rights reserved. No part of this publication may be reproduced, distributed, or transmitted in any form or by any means, including photocopying, recording, or other electronic or mechanical methods, without the prior written permission of the author, except in the case of brief quotations embodied in critical reviews and certain other non-commercial uses permitted by copyright law. For permission requests, write to the author at the address below.

ISBN: 978-0-578-99224-2 (Paperback)

Published by:

Emily Quintero-Spongberg– A Positive Image Ministries
316 Georgetown Drive
Glastonbury, CT 06033
www.apositiveimage.com

Editorial Consultant: Anna Wiles
Front cover art: Todd L. Thomas.
Cover design: Tim Spongberg
Book design by: Tim Spongberg & Emily Quintero-Spongberg.

Printed in the United States of America.

First printing 2021.

Dedication

To the love of my life, Tim. You are an incredible man and husband, Honey. Your heart displays Jesus' love for me in a way that encourages, supports and cares about me. I could not have done this without you, Love! Not in a million years!

To my beloved children—Annette, Sandie, Gabe and Allison. There are not enough words for me to express my love and gratitude to you all. Your support through the years, through the thick and the thin, has meant everything to me. I hope I have done you proud!

To Bishop Terry Wiles, my Pastor and Mentor. Bishop, this book might not have happened if it weren't for your trust in me and asking me to teach. Your trust has had a profound impact on my life and I will always treasure that.

But most of all, to the absolute, without question, the Biggest, Truest and most Faithful love in all of my life, Jesus. Lord, without you I can do nothing! Thank you for your love, grace and the gift of expression. May your Holy Spirit use it to touch many—that will be my greatest reward. I love you so much Lord!

In Appreciation

I'm at a lack for words here! How can I ever adequately express my appreciation for such an unselfish giving of love, time and energy? My heart is full of gratitude for everyone of you. A huge thanks to all of you that I did not mentioned unintentionally—your prayers have been like a spear that has been weighted with the power of the Holy Spirit.

Again, Tim, for your many hours of reading and staying up late. You are an incredible artist, your illustrations inside the book are amazing! You inspire me and give me wings—therefore, I fly! I love!

To Anna Essick-Wiles who spent hours in her busy schedule to edit this book and make sure my grammar and punctuation were correct. Anna, you're making me a better writer.

To my friends who always inspire me to write and teach—Yanira Rivera, Ibelice Valentin, Laura Essick, Tracy Espada, Betsy De La Cruz and Sharon Gustave and Heather Spada, Cherie Charpentier, who spent their precious time reading each portion of the gear and for accepting to teach it. You're the best!

I would also like to thank my wonderful cheering squad—Brenda Dimmock, Lynette Espinosa who has waited for this book with great anticipation. To Natalia Liriano who held my feet to the fire by giving me a date I had to live up to.

To my ladies small group who have taught me more than I could ever teach them!

To my Leaders group, who show me that we're "better together."

Also, to the Daughters of Purpose Women's Ministry at my church, who love me for who I am and for their constant friendship, support and prayers. I love you all.

I truly hope that you will forgive me if I didn't mention you. There were so many wonderful supporters. I'm blessed.

Table of Contents

Introduction ·· 1

Section One—The Belt of Truth

Chapter 1	Wait a Minute ··························	9
Chapter 2	Why A Belt? ····························	13
Chapter 3	Are You For Real? ······················	15
Chapter 4	Standing? ·······························	21
Chapter 5	Where Is My Belt? ······················	25

Section Two – The Breastplate of Righteousness

Chapter 6	What Lies Beneath ·····················	33
Chapter 7	Do You Have It In My Size? ··········	39
Chapter 8	Just Put It On Girl ·····················	43

Section Three- The Shoes of Peace

Chapter 9	Look At Those Pretty Shoes ··········	53
Chapter 10	Going The Distance ····················	59
Chapter 11	If The Shoe Fits ························	63

Section Four – The Shield of Faith

Chapter 12	Forward March ·························	71
Chapter 13	Brace Yourself ··························	75
Chapter 14	Oiled And Ready To Go ···············	79

Section Five – The Helmet of Salvation

Chapter 15   The Battlefield ·················· 89
Chapter 16   Protection Guaranteed ············ 93
Chapter 17   One Size Fits All ················ 99
Chapter 18   Putting On The Helmet ··········· 103

Section Six – The Sword of the Spirit

Chapter 19   Two Sides To Everything ········· 113
Chapter 20   Hand To Hand Combat ············ 117
Chapter 21   Get A Grip ······················ 121
Chapter 22   To The Hilt ····················· 125
Chapter 23   Use It or Lose It ················ 129

Section Seven – The Seventh Weapon ········· 133

The Beginning ···························· 139

About the Author ························· 141

Introduction

There are several books out there on spiritual warfare. Most are well written and their authors are Believers who understand this topic very well. some are experts in the field of spiritual warfare.

We've been taught from our Pastors and Teachers about the armor of God and how it's the holy weaponry given to us by God so that we would be able to stand in the day battle.

But how does this relate to you and me? I have asked myself this same question many times. Every time I asked the Lord this question, I sensed the same answer, "no one has heard your side of it."

I was asked by my Pastor to teach a class on Sunday mornings. I was taken back a bit since he did not give me a specific theme or book he wanted me to teach. He left it up to me.

I spent a few weeks praying and studying the Word and asking the Lord to give me insights into His Word. I needed a message that would help women live their lives empowered by the Spirit of God.

During my times of prayer and study, I found myself stumbling on Ephesians 6—the armor of God. I don't mean to make light of the Bible when I say stumbling but I ran into it several times on my way to another Scripture. I realized that God was trying to tell me something about this particular chapter. I rested there on those verses. I pitched my tent at Ephesians 6 and began what has now been an eleven year journey writing this book.

During these eleven years my weaponry has been tested more than once in various arenas of my personal life—everything from family to ministry and even my personal walk with the Lord has been put to the test.

So with so many books out there on the topics of spiritual warfare and the armor of God, why would I want to write another book on the same subject? God told me to do it. When God tells you to do something in that Father tone of His, you do it.

I began to research and realized that there were no books on this particular topic written specifically for the women of our time. These are tumultuous and vicious times—Satan wars fiendishly against our souls because he knows his time is running out.

It is my sincere prayer that as you read the pages of this book that you not only laugh but that you will come to have a better understanding of the full armor of God and that you would "put it on" so that you will be able to stand in the day of trouble.

I would like for us to go on a journey together. Let's look a bit more in depth into the need we have as women of God to be fully armed and dangerous.

There have been times when I neglected to put on the gear and I forfeited the protection it brings. I found myself in the middle of a battlefield alone, defenseless and bewildered.

Introduction

Satan has launched many attacks on me but I thank the One who fights my battles, our Holy Man of War, our Feared Champion who even in those times when I neglected my weapons came to my rescue time and time again.

I'd like to tell you that I always start my days in clad in complete armor but the *cares of this world* soon cause me to neglect that which is of most importance for my daily victory.

Jesus loves us unconditionally—He understands the struggles and challenges we face. I always want to do the right thing but I don't, I don't want to do the wrong things, but I do (… Paul).

My desire is to serve Him and to follow Him faithfully until the end. Jesus said "without Me you can do nothing (Ephesians 4:13) but in His awesome love, He provided for us all that we would ever need not only to stay in the battle, but to win it.

My daily war is not against an enemy I scan ee but against an evil ruler who hates me. Sometimes it's against the opinions I have of myself or it can be my present circumstances. At times, it is about health or loved ones or personal finances—these bring fear to my heart.

Fear is a deadly weapon and Satan knows how to wield it expertly to bring me down. Depression and discouragement are booby traps along the way that rob me of peace.

There are many things that set themselves up against my soul to cause me to stumble and fall into that deadly pit where Satan wants me to fall into so he can devour me.

Whether my battle is against the world, my flesh or the devil, I know Jesus has secured my victory through the holy weaponry provided for me by Christ. Everyday will be filled with challenges until I go to see Him face to face, but He gave me the armor I need so that when the enemy hurls his attacks on me I will be able to stand.

My prayer is that by the end of this book, you will be reminded of the great measure of the love of Christ and how much he protects those He loves. I stand with you in this battle, cheering you on to victory, a fellow warrior.

Emily Spongberg

Section One

The Belt of Truth

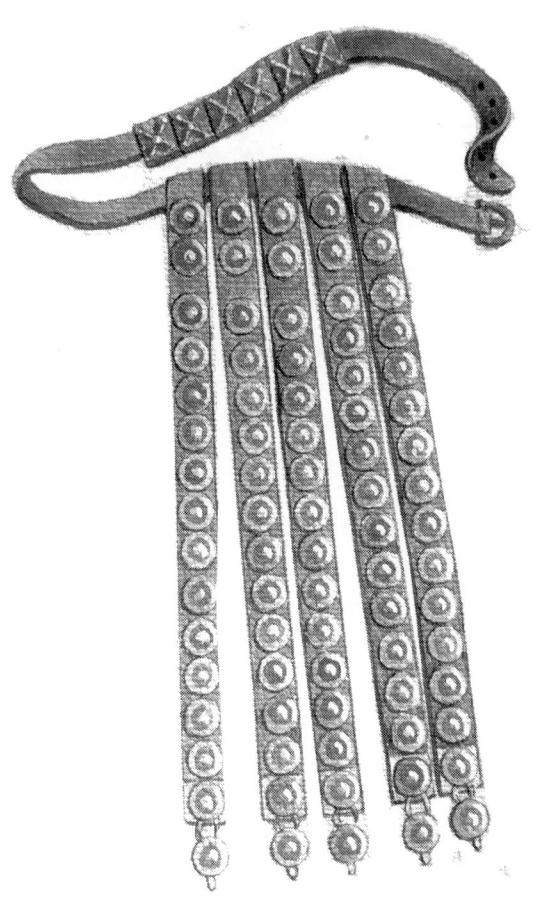

Chapter One

Wait a Minute

"Stand firm then, with the belt of truth buckled around your waist..." (Ephesians 6:14)

The belt is an overlooked fashion accessory. It follows fashion trends, but it doesn't seem to be as prominent as jewelry, handbags or shoes. Yet, it can have as much a place over the final look of an outfit as any other accessory.

A belt is sometimes necessary to pull an outfit together; it can be understated but still add elegance to an outfit or it can be the WOW factor. Either way, the right belt has something to say.

Sometimes we see a dress we really like but when we try it on, something seems to be missing. Our faithful girlfriend, who is in the dressing room, observes the same thing.

"Wait a minute!" she says. She goes out and comes back with an array of belts in different colors and styles. "This will make that dress look fabulous on you."

You follow your friend's suggestion and after trying on a few belts, you put on the one that seems to have been left out of the ensemble. It is a perfect match and the perfect completion to your outfit. Your friend is feeling very accomplished and says, "**girl, you're dressed to kill.**"

I miss wearing belts. I once had a closet full, ranging in colors reflecting the statement each belt would make. Whether with slacks and a tucked shirt or over a top for an evening or dinner I had a belt. I wish I could wear belts again but after a surgery that scarred my waistline, I am no longer able to wear them. I still love them and often stop at the belt rack to see what's in and to just admire them. Maybe someday I will be able to wear them again.

Perhaps you are wondering what all this has to do with the armor of God and the belt of truth? Good question. I would be asking the same thing if I were reading this chapter for the very first time. But bear with me.

First, let's talk about the belt worn by the Roman soldier. The Latin word for the belt was the "Cingulum Militaire" (Military Belt.) Unlike the belt I just described, this belt was not a fashion statement, even though it had some military adornments added by the soldier. It were decorated with studs or coins gained in wars they fought. These coins and metal studs were placed both on the belt and the attached straps to add beauty. They also added additional protection.

The soldier's belt was worn firmly around his waist; it was a vital piece of the armor made of leather. The leather was treated with a special tanning method that would harden it. This process made the belt rigid and firm so that it would fit properly around the soldier's waist. This was not the type of belt you tilt to one side to create some asymmetry and style, but it was a necessary tool on which to hang all the other parts of the armor.

What does truth have to do with it?

In Ephesians 6:14, the Apostle Paul starts out with the number one piece of the armor, the belt of truth. The belt is considered a defensive weapon.

We wouldn't think of a belt as a defensive weapon, but Paul, while observing the Roman soldier he was chained to, noticed the belt and begins to describe it as "the belt of truth."

Even though it was not necessary for the soldier he was attached to have all his armor while guarding Paul, he would have been wearing his belt. Paul was a Roman citizen as well as a Jewish Rabbi. He was very familiar with the Roman soldier his weaponry. He was very schooled in the ways of war and the weaponry needed to win the battle.

Paul understood and knew from experience that the Roman soldier was an elite fighting machine.

They were not just trained to fight to the death but they were feared through the then known world.

Chapter Two

Why a Belt?

"...you will know the truth, and the truth will set you free." (John 8:32)

The soldier wore a red woolen tunic underneath his weaponry. The belt kept the tunic in place and allowed the soldier to pull the tunic up and run when necessary.

1Peter 1:13 commands us to "gird up." This Greek word is (zŏnnymi) which means to take out the slack, raise up a tunic properly, be ready for action. We are then to gird our minds and hearts with the truth of Christ Jesus who said "I am... the Truth." (John 14:6

Jesus is the truth, in Him there is no lie, no discrepancy, no hiding of what is real. There is no shadow of truth but He is the Truth. The truth should be clad to us like the belt was to the Roman soldier. Without his belt, the soldier was left weaponless and powerless. Without truth, God's truth, we are also left defenseless and incapable to fight our very powerful enemy, Satan.

In Biblical times, men and women wore a long dress like tunics, but wore a sash or belt tied around the waist so that if the person needed to run or avoid obstacles, they would pull the tunic up over the belt as needed to prevent stumbling or falling.

We have to put on that truth and apply the Word to our lives and live it out. We are to display Christ by the way we live. John the Baptist said when he declared Jesus was the lamb of God, "I must decrease that He may increase." What an amazing statement to live by.

The belt is the primary piece of the armor because everything hangs on it. Imagine having to carry all those weapons without having something to hold them. It would be impossible for the soldier. His arms and hands would be all tied up and he would not be able to defend himself against his enemy who is very equipped to bring his prey down.

So too it is with our spiritual belt. The belt of truth represents our living out our lives in Christ with integrity, honesty and transparency; a life that displays an impeccable character, Godliness and represents Jesus who is "all Truth."

Chapter Three

Are You for Real?

"...thou desirest truth in the inward parts:..."
(Psalm 51:6 KJV)

Have you ever come across a person who claims to be one thing but displays something else before others? They may say that they live a life of integrity but their actions don't support that.

If we don't live a life that is based on truth, we will be like that defeated soldier that has nothing to hang his weapons on. He will not be able to overpower his enemy. He will become ineffective and his life will be at great at risk.

So truth is the "absolute Word of God" by which we are clothed. It is the absolute truth of His Scripture by which we must live. And if we live by that absolute truth, then we can't be one person saying one thing and doing another.

Truth makes its way to the light. Jesus also said, "I am the Light of the World." He was not hidden from us, but He revealed Himself to the world. He *is* the pure light of God, He is God. He also spoke of a city on a hill, giving light and also about how a lamp could not be hidden but would give off its light.

Peter admonishes us that we are to gird up the loins of our minds so that when we need to take action, based on God's truth and not the world's brand of truth, we are ready for action.

The belt though common and not particularly a show stopper, was crucial because it held all the other weapons in place.

If we live our lives with spiritual integrity, then the world will see the results of the Holy Spirit residing in us as we bring glory and honor and the testimony of Christ's power dwelling in us.

Our walk for God and in the Spirit is perfected as we build our knowledge of His Word and apply it to our lives. We are therefore able to labor for Christ with visibility and effectiveness. *(2 Timothy 3:17, NIV)*

In Ephesians 6:11, Paul commands us to "put on the full armor of God, so that you can take your stand against the devil's schemes."

The word "scheme or schemes" means to make plans, especially in a devious way or with the intent to do something illegal or wrong. Our enemy the Devil never stops with his manipulating, planning and ideas to bring us down. But the command says we are to put on the whole the armor, in all its entirely not omitting any part.

However, the belt is the supporting piece. There is no

putting on the full armor without it. The Word of Truth must reside in us as we are diligent to search, study, understand and apply it to our hearts daily.

God's Word is the vein of our spiritual existence. We are helpless against those fiery darts that Satan will continuously hurl against us.

We must put on the whole armor. It starts with truth. The Scriptures are uncompromising, there is no area for bargaining with the Holy Spirit on accepting only what pleases us or gives claim to our own pleasures. It's all or nothing! The Lord will not allow us to be half-hearted. Truth is the absolute element of our spiritual heart and life and how we live it.

Satan laughs and mocks a believer who has loosened his/her belt allowing the rest of the armor to fall off. He has a field day with our hearts and minds and will render us ineffective and powerless.

Since the truth is found in God's Word, we need to be firmly planted and secure in what it teaches us. Without the belt (truth) there can be no breastplate of righteousness, no protection against an impure heart and its lustful desires. We will not be able to accept that it is not we ourselves that make us righteous, but the blood and sacrifice of Jesus Christ because He is our righteousness.

Without the belt there are no shoes of peace. Our shoes of the peace of the Gospel are loose, untied and insecure and we are not able to go out with preparation of the Word and the conviction that we need in order to reach this dying world for Jesus and make disciples.

Without the belt, we can't wield our swords and find protection behind the shield against the onslaught of the evil one when he tries to blow us out of the water with his lies.

God's Word says, that "no weapon forged against you will prevail…" (Isaiah 54:17 – NIV).

If we stop and consider this often-misquoted scripture, we come to understand that Satan also has mighty weaponry that he uses against the Believer. He forges, (Greek verb sfyrilato which means to hammer. To pound on.)

Our enemy hammers out his weapon against us like an iron smith banging on that hot iron making an effective weapon. He deploys lies, temptations, lust, greed and insecurity about God's love and grace against us. He keeps us from a healthy spiritual life by distracting us from the Bible and time with the Lord thereby convincing us to follow his ways.

When we neglect the health of our daily time with God, we become easy prey. So, we are commanded to be skillful with the Word of God in our warfare. Paul wrote to the young Timothy, "Do your best to present yourself to God as one approved, a worker who correctly handles the word of truth. (2 Tim 2:15)

There are a few key words that are sometimes overlooked in this verse. First is the word "study." Studying requires effort, determination, dedication and hard work. It is an attitude that we are going to delve into a topic and learn all we can about it. It requires a studious mindset.

When we apply this to our study of the Bible, we become that disciple, that leader Paul was talking about, unashamed and approved by God. We find truth in what we understand and believe about God and His mighty Word.

Satan can certainly cause us to feel shame in a hurry. In fact, he delights in it. His goal is to confuse us as to what is and isn't truth.

It is very important that we interpret God's Word with integrity of mind and seek out what God is really saying with the help of the Holy Spirit and not look for a false truth that merely gives credence to our own fleshly desires. God is not a liar and what He says in His Word is exactly what He means. No exceptions!

Chapter Four

Standing

"The Lord will fulfill his purpose for me..."

(Psalm 138:8) KJV)

We can become spiritually bankrupt if we are not diligent to feed our minds and heart with continual truth, understanding exactly what the Word is saying is of the highest importance. This is why Paul tells us to "stand" 3 times in Ephesians 6. We must stand on God's Word and only His Word. His Word is Truth.

Hosea 4:1 says that "God's people are destroyed for lack of knowledge." Our understanding should be that we need understanding and knowledge in order to obtain wisdom. We need knowledge about what the Lord desires of us and what He has done for us. In doing so we learn to   live the successful, Godly life we are expected and commanded to live.

If we have no knowledge of God and who He is through His Word, then we will lack the information and experience we need to be a competent and powerful soldier. It is not enough to learn a few verses and quote them when needed. When we feel Satan breathing down our necks. We need to understand and know what they mean and how Holy Spirit wants to affect our spirits through it.

Many times, we take Scripture out of context to suit our present situation or heart condition. When this happens, our belts are not cinched and they fall off our waists. We are not properly girded with the truth, we are unable to understand what it means to have the breastplate of righteousness, the helmet of salvation, the shield of faith, and the sword of the Spirit, God's Word.

It is our privilege and duty to immerse ourselves in God's holy and beautiful Word. We will be able to become like that tree that is planted by the water: strong, giving shade to those who need shelter from the heat of life. (Jeremiah 17:7-8 NIV)

So, what keeps our belts from being properly fixed around our hearts? I can't think of a better question right now. We can consider Jesus parable of the Sower where He compares the seed to His Word. (Matthew 13:1-9, 18 -23, NIV.) In this parable, Jesus makes the distinction between an unhealthy and a healthy seed.

Some seed fell on rocky soil and eaten by the birds, a person who hears the Truth but it does not take root in his heart. This type of seed does not take hold of the ground so that it is able to root and grow. If our hearts lack good, healthy and deep soil, the Devil will descend on us and devour the seed that God has planted, His Word.

Some seed fell on rocky ground and even though it rooted some and came up, it quickly died because its roots were not deep enough and fell victim to the heat of the day. Some hearers of the Word are like that, they hear the Gospel, they go up to answer the invitation to follow Christ. But the seed has not penetrated the soil enough. It took some root but when they find themselves struggling the heat of the battles of life, they uproot themselves and do not survive because of their shallow roots.

As I said earlier, sometimes we select some choice verses, take them out of context and make a theology out of them. We then align ourselves to those lies that the enemy of our souls would throw at us. Because we have not applied truth, exposing our lack of knowledge, our seed can germinate and look pretty for a while but as Jesus said when the cares of this world come, the seed dies.

What a beautiful thing it is to see a Believer that flourishes and grows bringing hope to others, like that tree planted by the water whose leaves bring comfort from the heat of life to others in despair. God's Word, the belt on which everything we believe and are hangs on, causes this effect in the hearts of those who observe our holy walk.

Colossians 3:16 is like a directional needle that points us in the right direction. "Let the message of Christ dwell among you richly…" This Word, Holy Seed must dwell deeply within us so that we can become effective disciples for the Lord Jesus Christ.

When the Holy Spirit takes up residence in our hearts and remains there, we are able to stay on course thereby keeping our belts securely tied so that we can confidently hang everything else on it. The World and the Body of Christ will benefit from such a life.

If we feel un-righteous and un-deserving then our breastplate is not hanging on the belt, it has fallen off. Doubting our salvation means that we have no place on which to hang our helmets.

The Bible re-enforces our identity in Christ, but if we are not sure that we have been saved by God's grace, we will not be able to keep our helmets on.

I love what David says in Psalm 119:11,

"I have hidden your Word in my heart that I may not sin against you." NIV)

He hides it as the most treasured possession of his life. Even though he was the wealthiest of kings, he found no worldly treasure greater than God's Word. He hid it so it would not be stolen from him. He had a strong hold on it so he would not only know it but that it would keep him from sinning against his God.

David loved God more than anything else or anyone on earth. Even though he committed a great sin, he longed to be forgiven and resume that relationship he had had with the Lord.

Chapter Five

Where's My Belt?

"Sanctify them by the truth; your word is truth."
(John 17:17)

It is vital, of the utmost importance, that we not cast off our belt, that we do not neglect searching and studying the Bible as it is our life, our breath, the very marrow of our bones, the substance of life. This belt of truth will allow us to live in this world in victory for Christ allowing us to smash all the vicious lies that the Devil may hurl against us to bring us down.

The strips of leather that hung from the belt were there to protect the soldier's groin area. If the soldier was injured in this area, not only would he be ineffective in the battle, but it could also prevent him from fathering children. Family was very important in the Roman culture. Even though their children were not large in number due to infantile deaths, they still valued their offspring that would also ensure the continuance of their generations.

Believers should also be concerned about protecting our ability to birth spiritual children for God's kingdom.

The Holy Spirit has planted in us that desire and ability to reproduce, multiply. We do this by displaying Christ in us by the way we live.

As Christians, we cannot allow ourselves to become spiritually impotent to the point that we don't reproduce for God. Just as He commanded Adam and Eve to be fruitful and to multiply, so does He with us. Our fruitfulness comes from a life led by the Spirit of God, our multiplication is a result of that fruitfulness. Jesus said that we were to bear much fruit for Him (John 14). By living a fruitful life, one that produces much fruit, we are able to increase God's Kingdom with spiritual, born again, Spirit filled, fully devoted followers of Christ. We do this by living a life that exemplifies Jesus in us and we in Him.

Jesus' statement in the Gospel of John that He is the Truth is quite astounding. He is the Word incarnate, God in human form come to live among His creation by becoming a man and living among His creation so that He might forgive the world of sin and save us.

He is the Logos, the Alive Word of God, the Power of God's Word. By His Word, all things that are were created. He created by the authority of His voice and command.

Christ is the Holy Seed, the incorruptible seed that was to come and crush Satan, disrobe him of all he stole from mankind, bring him down and show him that he was powerless and that he had no dominion over Him (Jesus).

Our need to put on the belt is a holy duty, to a holy God who has called us to be His holy army. As we study His Word and make every effort with Holy Spirit to study it so that He can give us the understanding and with the Word that comes forward from our Pastors teachings, we are on our way to becoming a soldier that is truly "dressed to kill"

Section Two

The Breastplate of Righteousness

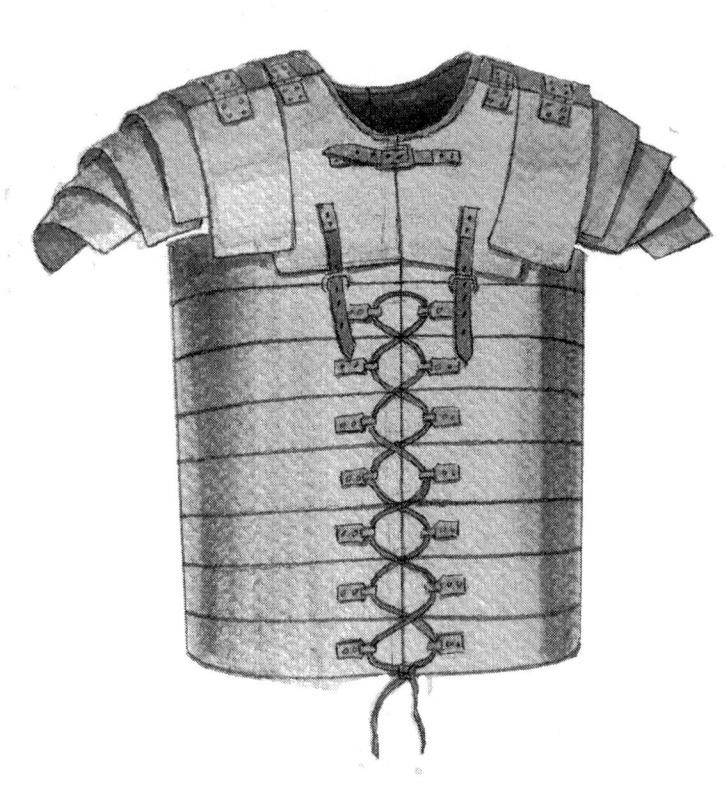

Chapter Six

What Lies Beneath

"Stand firm then... with the breastplate of righteousness in place..." (Ephesians 6:14)

In the ancient world, one of the most crucial parts of a soldier's arsenal was his breastplate. Even though it was for the soldier's protection during battles, the breastplate was second to none in both beauty and design.

The Latin name for this part of the military suit was the "lorica segmentata." It was shaped like a shell and covered the soldier from the neck down and to the top of the knee.

The breastplate was made out of brass scale-like pieces and held together with metal loops that were as cut to size and had holes at the top so that it could be attached with metal rings to leather straps around the body. When it was completely assembled, they looked like a garment made out of fish scales.

Though sturdy and weighing in at approximately 18 pounds, the legionnaires could move swiftly and with great agility in a hand-to-hand combat situation. The shoulders were fitted in such a way that the soldier could be flexible and was able to wield his sword and shield with great agility. It was also easily put away when not in use because it was made of four pieces that were connected by rings at the shoulders and sides.

Even though this was a weapon of war, the chest piece was amazingly beautiful. The enemy couldn't miss them as they came into view. This spectacle must have created dread and fear in the hearts of their enemy.

So why am I talking to you about all this Roman equipment? What does that have to do with spiritual warfare and God's armor? Bear with me Sister, bear with me and I will show you what Paul saw that caused him to write this sixth chapter in his letter to the Ephesians.

The Bible has much to say about our heart. It calls it wicked, easily misled, it bows to other gods and is quick to follow the lust of the flesh.

Genesis 3 records the account of our first parents' sinful choice to follow the great deceiver. Satan manipulated Eve into thinking that she could be like God, Hum, sounds familiar? I recall reading in Ezekiel how Satan was cast out of Heaven for the very same thing. Isaiah also records his willfulness and rebellion against the Lord.

The offering of the fruit from the tree of good and evil was tempting to Eve so she ate of it and offered it to her husband, opening up a world of decay and corruption that was never meant for us to experience. This was the pivotal moment that separated mankind from his Creator.

This story didn't end in tragedy and death, however, the same Creator that Adam and Eve sinned against came to their defense quickly. The biblical account in this third chapter of Genesis goes on to say that they were so ashamed that they made coverings out of fig leaves and hid in the bushes when they heard God calling out to them.

I always want to cry when I read this. I can almost hear the Lord calling out to them in that wonderful Fatherly tone, "Adam, where are you." God knew exactly where they were but they needed to confess what they had done. Their sin of rebellion, disobedience and pride had separated them from the Lord.

I love how the Lord came looking for them. He does the same with us. But I'm really moved when it says that the Lord killed an innocent animal to make them a covering made with His own hand—not one by Adam or Eve's hand, which would rot and decay the next day as the fig leaves would, but a covering that could not be destroyed or removed by Satan.

Jesus, the Lamb of God, laid Himself down on that cross so that we could become righteous again. We are covered forever, not by our own design and making, but by a covering made for us through the blood of His Son.

In the same way that the shield protected the fighter, we are also protected by Jesus' righteousness. But where do we get that righteousness? Paul said that, *"This righteousness from God comes through faith in Jesus Christ to all who believe." (Romans 3:22)*

So our right standing, our righteousness, comes from God. He is the only one who can make it possible for you and I to be approved once again.

Our hearts need protection. Just like the soldier was protected from the weapons of his enemy, so we are protected by the blood of Christ. When we believe and accept Him as the Lord of our hearts, we become righteous and are in right standing with our Creator.

Wow! That's amazing, I can't explain exactly how that happens but I know one thing, when I turned my life over to God, I felt like a brand-new person; so clean and pure. It's as if I had just been born. And I had.

Do you remember the day that you became acceptable before the Lord, born again? Perhaps you felt like I did; fresh and clean, like you could go straight to Heaven. What great joy that was. Jesus said that there is great rejoicing among the angels in Heaven when a sinner comes back to God. What a party Girls!

But it wasn't very long before we strayed from that Heavenly bliss and went on to serve other gods. You know, the god of me, myself and I. The one that we put first above all other things. It doesn't take long for us to make ourselves a covering hoping that God won't notice so we go and hide behind a bush.

We have to trade in our righteousness for His. Jesus' garment will not become old nor decay like our parent's fig leaves. This covering of our hearts is for all eternity. If you mess up, get up, confess and straighten out your breastplate and keep on fighting!

Chapter Seven

Do You Have That In My Size?

"Keep thy heart with all diligence; for out of it are the issues of life." (Proverbs 4:23)

Webster's dictionary defines "righteous" as acting in accordance with divine or moral law: free from guilt or sin. It also describes it as one who is upright and virtuous—a person of good character. That is Mr. Webster's wonderful description of the word righteous.

The Bible has much to say about righteousness and the heart of man. It says that the heart is wicked and that no man can know it. Jesus teaches us to guard our hearts because all life's issues proceed from it.

In Matthew 2:28, the Lord spoke to those who appeared to be righteous on the outside but were wicked on the inside. Righteousness can be observed by our fellow man and it can appear to us that some people, because they live a good life, that they are righteous in the eyes of the Lord. But God is the only

One who can truly judge a person's righteousness because He's the only One who can look deep into our hearts and discern our true motives and condition.

Proverbs 4:23 says, "above all, guard your heart..." Our hearts can certainly deceive us if we don't keep our emotions in check. They will get the best of us if we are not careful to protect them from the oncoming ammunition that Satan can throw at them. We have to be careful not to allow unforgiveness and strife to take residence, these emotions can be our downfall.

If man's heart is wicked, as the Bible says, how can we ever hope to reach a point of righteousness that will please God? Our hearts need to be examined constantly. But am I capable of looking deep within? We can certainly know and correct our hearts if we rely on God's Holy Spirit to show us their condition and the areas that need attention.

King David knew the importance of allowing God to show him the condition of his heart. He says in Psalm 139:23,

"Search me, O God, and know my heart: try me, and know my thoughts..." (KJV)

David had not forgotten how easy it was for his heart to become ensnared by sin. His eyes lusted over what was not his to have and he fell into sin and his close relationship with God was grieved. He realized that only God could see his soul. The Bible tells us that he was a man after God's own heart. Oh, my! I would love to have that said about me.

Unfortunately, when we take our sights off of the Lord, we are doomed to fail just as David did. No one of us that has ever lived on this earth can ever say that they weren't blindsided by sin. We are all capable of this. We can never see our hearts for what they truly are. We cannot see the decay of our hearts unless we offer them to God, just as they are, with humility and repentance and God, our Father, will restore us through His Son, Jesus.

The Breastplate that the Lord provides for us is capable of keeping us shielded from spiritual death. When we came to Christ, we were all provided that same righteousness that was given to Peter, John and all those who would lay down their lives to follow Him.

Since Jesus is our righteousness, we know that there are no varying degrees of righteousness, we were made righteous.

"...but ye are washed, but ye are sanctified, but ye are justified in the name of the Lord Jesus, and by the Spirit of our God."
(1 Corinthians 6:11)

Chapter Eight

Just Put It On Girl!

*'I desire to do your will, my God; your law is within my **heart**." (Psalm 40:8)*

In the verse above, we can hear David's love for God and his desire to please Him; God was his breath and life. What is not said but can be understood here is that he knew he was righteous in God's eyes.

It was this knowing that he was in right standing with God that caused David to have this intimate friendship with his Lord. He also knew that this wasn't due to anything that he had done, but it was everything that God had done. He had the vision in his heart about the coming Savior.

The only time we hear his troubled heart about his broken relationship with Gof is in Psalm 51. David had sinned against God with Bathsheba. It was at this time that we hear a heart that is not guilt ridden but repentant. David felt the absence of the Lord's presence and he knew exactly what caused the wall that he built between God and himself.

But do we see ourselves in the same way David did regarding his righteousness? I dare say no. We have such a hard time accepting that our relationship with the Father is not because of what we do or don't do, it's about what He did. He sent His precious Son to this fallen world for us. This is what it's all about Friends, this is what it's all about.

There is no greater pleasure to the Devil than for us to feel that we are not good enough for God, and he would be right in that. However, the truth is that we are righteous in Christ Jesus. Satan knows that too but he works hard at convincing us otherwise.

Dear ones, you are in right-standing with God, of course you are. When our Heavenly Father looks down at us He doesn't see our old sinful selves, oh no, He sees you through the blood of Christ that covers you. That is what makes us righteous, in right-standing with Him.

Jesus' loving and unselfish sacrifice gave us the right to put on that breastplate once we receive Him into our hearts and surrender our lives to Him completely.

Note that I said completely, there is no half-hearted way to accepting that God loves you because you love His Son. There can't be any wavering, that would be doubt, wouldn't it? If we accept Jesus' sacrifice and understand why He came, then we have to accept this righteous covering provided for us at Calvary.

> "This righteousness is given through faith in Jesus Christ to all who believe..." (Romans 3:22)

I don't know about you my sister, but that clinches it for me. When Satan tries to make me look at my past mistakes and sinful behavior, I throw this verse back at him. I make sure that my breastplate is tight and secure. No wounds inflicted here, no way!

Remember how I started by explaining how this part of the gear looked like fish scales? They were very close together in order to provide the protection the soldier needed.

The reason the breastplate was the most beautiful of the armor pieces was due to the radiance that it had. The reason for this was that the scales would rub against each other and create a luster, that luster made it glow, especially out in the open. This must have been a sight to see!

Imagine how we must glow before God and others when we have our breastplate on and correctly fastened. The assurance that we have been made right before our Father causes us to glow, shine. Our very confidence in that truth causes us to be what we were created for, servants of the Almighty Creator; here to do His will at His beckoning.

I love my church's mission statement, it says;

"We exist to follow the teaching of the scriptures in reaching people with the gospel of Jesus Christ and helping them to become fully devoted followers of Jesus Christ..."(Mission statement for Crossroads Community Cathedral, East Hartford, CT.)

But how can we do that? If we are waffling in how we

view our standing with God, we will not be able to convince another person that they are made right with God through Christ Jesus.

The interesting thing to note about the scales in the Roman breastplate was that it was the pieces rubbing together that created its radience. I believe that this relates to the Church working together to accomplish Christ's mission to build His Church.

"As iron sharpens iron, so one person sharpens another." (Proverbs 27:17)

No one likes to work with a dull knife. Have you ever seen a chef or cook sharpening their knife? Perhaps you've done it yourself. I have a knife sharpener that does exactly what this verse says. The iron pieces rubbing on the knife take away it's dullness and make it sharp again. I love a sharp knife; it allows me to do exactly what I need it to do.

When we allow another to come to us in love and give us counsel and advice on something they have observed that goes against the person we are becoming, we need to trust that. The Bible says that:

"Wounds from a friend can be trusted..."
(Proverbs 27:6)

I will always be grateful for those sincere friends and mentors in my life who had enough love for me and courage to tell me things they had observed that needed to be changed. It's not easy to receive correction. We get that knee jerk reaction and our hackles go up. It is one of those moments that we find ourselves in battle. The flesh rises up and we might feel angry with our friend or receive it as criticism. Perhaps we might feel that they are no longer on our side.

This counsel in Proverbs is great advice, one that may be hard to apply at the moment of correction but one that is necessary if the iron is going to sharpen the iron. This advice, if given in love and received in trust, will keep us on track to fulfilling our full purpose.

True friendship to me is a holy bond, it's a sacred alliance. If a friend comes to us because they love us and they want our character to shine, then we need to trust that their intention is not to hurt us but to protect us. I need those true friends, how about you?

Let me conclude with this, our breastplate must be worn if we are to survive this battle. Satan will pierce our hearts and do great damage. I'm not in any way saying that if you don't wear this breastplate you are not saved, heavens no. But what I *am* saying is that you will be needlessly wounded in the fight. This is not what the Lord wants for His Church. The Church is triumphant, victorious!

> *"Do not be afraid of them...for I have given you victory." (Joshua10:8 NLT)*

This Scripture wasn't meant just for Joshua, but for every believer in Christ. We, too, are in a battle against Satan and his fiendish allies. We have crossed over to the side and the Devil no longer has a hold on us.

Remember Ladies, that we may have battles to fight until we go to our Heavenly home, but our Commander in Chief, Jesus won the war. He gave us this victory at the Cross and that is our victory. So, receive it. Put on that breastplate and live victorious!

Section Three

The Shoes of Peace

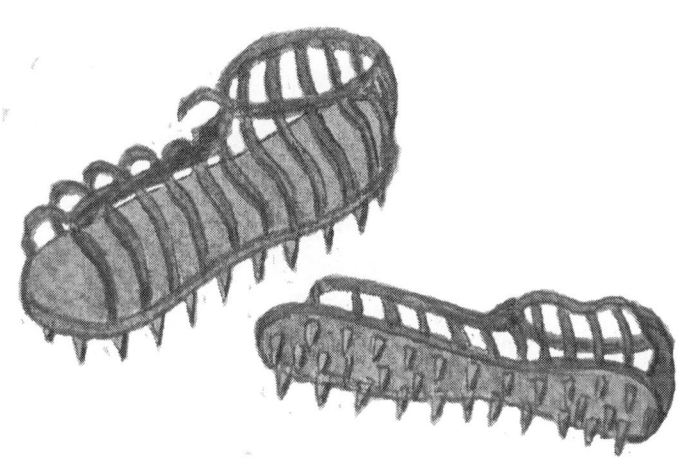

Chapter Nine

Look At Those Pretty Shoes

"And your feet shod with the preparation of the gospel of peace..." (Ephesians 6:15 KJV)

I have to tell you upfront Girls that I'm going to be talking about shoes again. *I know!* But don't worry, these shoes don't rot in an unbreathable box like the last pair I shared with you. Neither are they red or high heeled. You might be thinking right about now "how boring"—no color and no heels, what then? They have a happy ending!

In the verse above in Ephesians 6:15 Paul puts the shoes third in his line-up of the spiritual armor. He instructs (commands us) to ready ourselves by putting on the shoes of peace. What do shoes have to do with the armor of God? We are going to delve into this little fashion nugget here and see what our brother Paul has to say about shoes. But first, a little history; we don't want to leave our Roman military friend behind do we?

The Roman wars were long. The legionnaire was superbly trained and disciplined to endure the hardships of war and the rough terrain they would travel on. The soldiers faced sickness, impairment, hunger and sadly, the loss of comrades. The soldiers could be gone for years at a time, missing their spouses and the experience of seeing their children grow.

Every piece of the armor was made for effect and durability. The troops couldn't stop at the next local shoe repair guy to have something fixed or re-made. The shoes were made to last and had to be durable enough protect the men from an injured foot.

The shoes were the only part of the Roman issue that was not affixed to the belt.

The shoes may not have appeared to be beautiful, fancy or made by the best shoe designers in the Roman Empire, but they were more important than the footwear worn by the common people or the aristocracy. Paul puts the shoes in the third place on the spiritual military wear lineup.

"And your feet shod with the preparation of the gospel of peace..." (Ephesians 6:15 KJV)

I feel terrible for those dear soldiers and how long and hard they had to walk. Let's face it, outside of Rome, the soldiers did not have had those well engineered, wide roads to march on.

The Roman soldier's shoes were strategically made. They protected the soldier's feet, be tough and durable but comfortable. This footwear was made of two separate parts to aid in all kinds of terrain and conditions.

Let's start with the sandals. *No*, nothing like our pretty summer sandals but far different. You will probably not like the ones I am about to describe.

The shoes were made of both metal and leather and had three inch spikes at the bottom of the soles. The metal parts were at the top of the foot for maximum protection. Imagine someone driving a spear on his foot or an arrow that had slidden off that well-oiled shield burning a hole into his foot.

Have you ever had a callous or a corn on your foot? It has to be one of the most awful things to deal with. You can't keep your mind off the pain when you try to put on shoes and walk around.

The metal, like the breastplate, was attached to the rest of the shoe which was made of hardened leather. (I discuss this process in more detail in the section about the shield.) It took several layers and water soaking to make them hard.

But why does Paul use such strong words like "shod" to describe putting on the shoes. *Shod?* I want to use the King James translation of this word because it has more impact for me. (Remember those horses)

The word "shod" is a common word used in respect to horses. A horse is put through this process in order to protect it from rough terrains and exposure to nails, stones or wood slivers that could burrow themselves into the horse's hooves. The process of shoeing or fitting a horse's hooves, helped the horse to hold his ground and keep him steady especially when he was carrying a rider. The shoes would help the horse to distribute the extra weight and keep it balanced.

The shoes worn by the Roman military had three inch spikes that were placed at the soles. The spikes allowed the soldier to fight on mountainous areas because he could dig those spikes into the hard ground and keep himself balanced—they also served as an additional weapon when thrust into the head of an opponent that was trying to climb the mountain to attack him.

Our spiritual shoes have spikes also, they are:

[22] ...the Spirit is love, joy, peace, longsuffering, gentleness, goodness, faith, [23] Meekness, temperance..." (Galatians 5:22 –23KJV)

We are able to drive those spikes into Satan's deceitful temptations by living in a manner that displays the fruit of God's Spirit living in us.

Many years ago, I lived on a farm in the Adirondack mountains and was blessed to own a few horses. Each of the horses was a different age and some were retired race horses. But no matter their age or background, one thing was for sure; that horse needed to be shod if it was going to ridden.

Even though they were experienced in carrying a rider, not putting shoes on them could cause an injury that could eventually go wrong and cost the animal his life. I know because such a thing happened to one of our most beloved horse.

When Paul commands us to be "shod" with the shoes, he is telling us to be prepared with the peace of the Gospel that brings a balanced life so when the extra weight of circumstances are laid upon us, we can maintain our spiritual posture without any danger of losing our ground.

You might not go out of your way to shoes like the ones I described, but you must. Just grab a hold of them Gals, you'll learn to appreciate them. In fact, you won't want to leave home without them.

Chapter Ten

Going The Distance!

"...And let us run with perseverance the race marked out for us..." (Hebrews 12:1)

Many years ago, I gave my heart, mind, body, soul and strength to God, I was just a young girl of fourteen. I had never heard that God loved me. I didn't know what it was like to be loved by anyone. I didn't know He cared. I felt that I was not acceptable to Him.

My opinion regarding God was that He was a lofty, uncaring, mean Being who just wanted to rule the World and that no matter what I did, it just wasn't enough.

What a bombastic lie! When you don't know any better, you fall for that way of thinking. I knew about God but I didn't know God, if I had, I would not have felt that way.

How many of us were caught up in that lie? We were tangled up in religion instead of a relationship with Christ—His way of life—a life completely surrendered to Him.

I want to tell you a story about a woman who lived in a

town called Samaria. The Jews did not usually associate with the Samaritans—they were considered by the Jews to be mongrels.

The conflict between the Jews and Samaritans went back to when the kingdom of Israel was divided into two nations. Israel, who was to the North had its own king while the tribe of Judah and half the tribe of Manasseh went to the South and became another kingdom, it too had its own king. Judah was the kingdom that David was king over and also the tribe that Jesus descended from. (See Matthew 1 for the Lord's genealogy)

For many generations the two kingdoms were against each other. Even though most of what the they believed was the same, there were some important discrepancies.

Through the years some religious organizations have tried to make this woman a prostitute. But nowhere in this account do we see anything that points to that. We are blessed to step back in time and listen to this conversation between Jesus and this woman. He asks her for water, she points out her gender and ancestry

When Jesus calls us, do we go into a tirade of how He couldn't possibly love us? We can't believe that He really loves or forgives us. How could He if I can't forgive myself for things I have done.

Jesus struck a nerve with this woman when He asked her to go get her husband. She had to fess up! She confesses that she doesn't have one. Jesus tells her all about her past five husbands and the current man in her life. Ouch! What do you do about now? Ladies, I don't know about you but I would've been asking that well to swallow me up!

The story doesn't go on to give us more dialogue between the woman and Jesus but only that she thinks He's a prophet. The argument stopped. She was no longer interested in the physical water. In fact, she asks Him for His water.

Right after that, (lets read between the lines and imagine the whole scenario) we read that *"she lay her pot down."* Her encounter with the Man at the well, whom she believed to be a prophet, arrested her soul. I believe that because she left her water pot behind, that it was at that moment that Sister had an encounter with the Liberator of her soul.

Her soul could not contain what she had experienced and what she was feeling at that moment. She had seen her Messiah, her Deliverer, her Hope. She felt clean, unjudged, accepted and fully known. This was an incredible moment for this fallen woman—a social pariah of sorts. A woman who was looked down on perhaps more by the women than the men—why would she be going to fetch water at a well at high noon in the fiercest heat of the day if not to avoid the jeers and whispers of the women folk.

This gal prepared herself through her admission that she was that woman that Jesus described. Not once does Jesus condemn her. His questions were meant to bring out the true condition of her soul so that He could forgive and transform her.

She finally understood about that living water because she was experiencing it. Ladies, those sandals she had on when she set off for the well, were not the same. Those shoes had fire in them—an urgency to go back and share with others what had just happened to her.

She couldn't contain the joy, she wanted others to come and see Him so that they would also drink the same water that Jesus had offered her.

The Samaritan woman's heart was fully prepared with the knowledge of what the Man said, but also His acceptance and what He had done for her. Sharing it was her joy.

The people believed her and went down to see Jesus. But hold up, what made them believe her? I think it was because the Holy Spirit empowered and changed her so that they no longer saw an immoral woman, but one that had been transformed.

Our Samaritan friend took a bold step forward. She believed Jesus. She left the false hopes and personal ambitions back in the water jug at the steps of a well that would only leave her thirsting again. So, in leaving her jug, the old was left behind. She prepared herself to run with the good news of the Gospel, she had great things to share and off she went!

Chapter Eleven

If The Shoe Fits

For as many of you as have been baptized into Christ have put on Christ. (Galatians 3:27 KJV)

I hope you enjoyed the story of the Samaritan woman. I feel as though I know her *(of course I never had 5 husbands and certainly I'm married to the one I have)* but just the way our sister at well, I have tried to shield myself from the Lord.

The Samaritan started her conversation with Jesus pointing out her lineage. She brings up her religion, her gender, and the social rules about men and women speaking to each other in public. She hoped that Jesus wouldn't start asking her about her personal life.

Hey, I don't always want to reveal to Jesus what I feel in my heart with words. I can come up with some pretty creative arguments myself. I try to guard my real thoughts and feelings with Him. My arguments become a protective shield that serve as a distraction to the real conversation Jesus and I need to have. Sound familiar?

Don't worry, we've all been there—we can feel shame or guilt or we just don't want to know what lurks inside a heart that we've neglected.

Words have power! Our words have the power to speak life or death.

Words kill, words give life; they're either poison or fruit—you choose. (Proverbs 18:21 The Message)

Our words can bring life to our hearts or we can be foolish and speak negative words about ourselves. We can speak words that reaffirm, heal, encourage and build not just ourselves, but others as well.

I remember reading an article about pots many years ago. I can't remember all that was said in this article but I do remember the point that it was trying to make. I was drawn to the phrase "leaky vessels,"—it had a strong implication about what we leave behind as we go through life—stinky stuff!

The woman at the well was transformed. She laid set that pot down and ran. She left behind all her negativity, her anger with those who treated her wrongly, her unforgiveness towards those husbands who perhaps had wronged her. Her heart was light, she could see a new beginning—and this my Friends is what motivated this woman to go! She's considered the Gospel's first missionary. How about that, Ladies!

So we have to put on this attitude that was in the Samaritan woman and leave our pot behind. Look fearlessly inside and see what it contains: insecurity, doubt, anger, poor self-esteem, self-hatred. I know that there are other things that perhaps you can add to this list. I know I can.

A regenerated heart inspires us to share this *Good News* we have received from above. Others did not keep from telling us how Great, Gracious and Merciful God was to them. We came to the light, and have great joy. Joy even in times of darkness and pain. The Word of God says that we have unspeakable joy when we come to Christ. This joy is not transitory like happiness which only lasts for a while, this is an eternal joy—one that we can experience now.

So if we have been received by God as His daughters through adoption through Jesus Christ, then like our sister at the well, we will leave all our shame and guilt at the feet of Jesus. She did and this very act enabled her to go and bring the Good News of the Gospel to her town.

There was no hesitation or thinking about it—it was spontaneous an it became an urgent matter to her. The pot with all the stinkiness in it —with all its cracks was no longer in her arsenal. She was able to bring the message of redemption to her town because she had been transformed, renewed, empowered and ready. She had prepared herself, she put on Christ and was ready to run! The Bible says:

How beautiful on the mountains are the feet of those who bring good news, who proclaim peace, who bring good tidings, who proclaim salvation, who say to Zion, "Your God reigns!" (Isaiah 52:7)

This verse says it all. We are never to be the bearer of bad news but of the good news that Jesus loves us and that He wants to transform our lives.

So, are you ready? Are you prepared to go share the Good News of the Gospel? *LET'S DO THIS!*

Section Four

The Shield of Faith

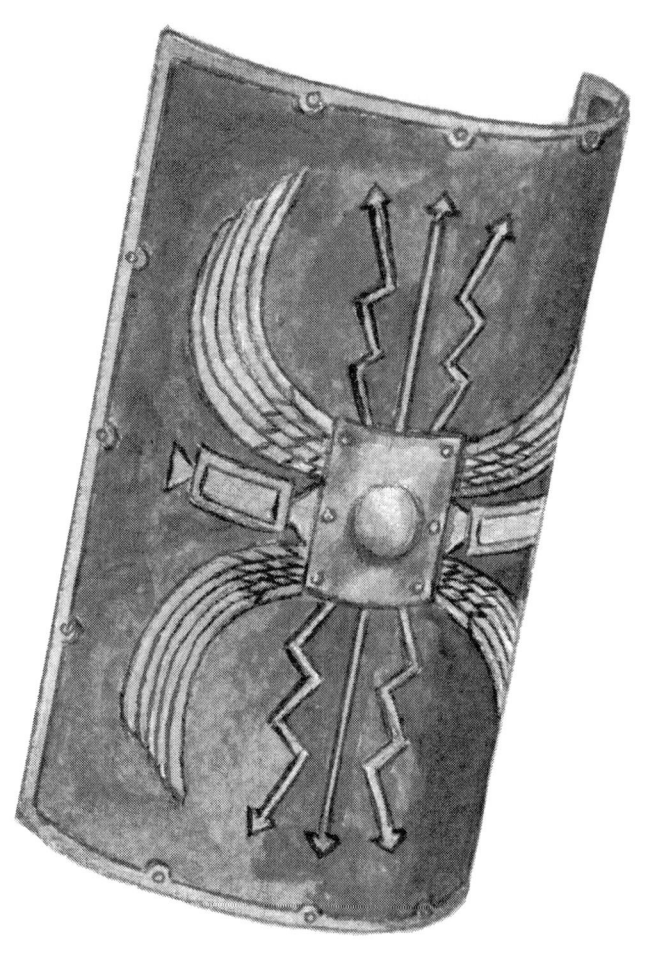

Chapter Twelve

Forward, March

"So then faith cometh by hearing, and hearing by the word of God." (Romans 10:17)

The Roman soldier had two shields, one was round and very stunning. This shield was simply for show in their parades and was not used in wars. This decorative shield would not have given the warrior the protection he needed.

The shield was a very essential weapon in the Roman legionary's arsenal. The shield used in battle was called the "scutum." It was long and wide and was called the door because that's what it looked like. It had a partly cylindrical shape that offered protection around part of the body.

In the middle of the outside portion of the shield, there was a steel ball called the "boss" where the handle came through to hang on the inside. The boss was really like an additional weapon. The soldier could thrust that shield so that the boss could knock out the opponent or at least put him off balance. The fighter was well trained in the use of his shield for maximum performance.

I know, you don't want to walk around with this cumbersome shield, right? I don't want to either, but the fact remains that we must. This shield in the spiritual arsenal is most essential. It is so essential that the Apostle Paul says above anything else, we need to hold up that shield in front of us.

The only way we can deflect those vile, dangerous bombs coming at us is through our faith. This shield is full body protection, a covering for the soul. Even though we don't literally carry a huge door-like shield as the Roman soldier did, we have a shield—which is our faith in God's Word.

When we believe and trust what Scripture says and trust that God will do what He says, then we become like a huge tank. We are like torpedoes and bombs blasting away at Satan and all his lies. We can do damage to the outside forces that want to destroy our faith.

Why does the Bible consider this such an important weapon? Imagine yourself out on a battlefield with no protection against oncoming blows and those deadly arrows that come against you out of nowhere. How do you protect yourself? You would be incapacitated quickly if your shield was away from you and not set in its right position in order to protect you.

One powerful verse says we need to have it at any and every battle that we face against the kingdom of darkness; it states, *"...with which you will be able to quench all the fiery darts of the wicked one." (Ephesians 6:16)* Think of a raging fire because that's exactly what happens when you are not guarded or if your shield has a crack or has become brittle. That arrow will explode on impact and you're down for the count. You might also bring some of your comrades down with you. Our faith is evident to others. We can either encourage them and help them to grow in faith or we can bring them down by our own lack of faith.

The arrows that the opposing forces hurled at the Roman army were not just plain old arrows. Ladies, they were loaded and ready to explode on impact. They were like those Molotov cocktails used in our day to create fires. The evil archer's goal is to penetrate your heart. But, if you are covered with your faith, there's no way this can happen. You have the complete protection through God's Word to be able to stand up to him. We have the power that we need to bring down strongholds and thoughts that want to linger and create attitudes and patterns that are sinfully destructive to our hearts if we ponder on them.

The care of our hearts is fundamental. When we stand on God's Word, we have the upper hand. The Scriptures have all the spears and swords we can throw back as a counter attack that will prevent any soul damage that can weaken us and keep us from winning those constant attacks.

The soldier knew how to care for his shield on a daily basis, his life depended on it. There was no question about its importance for him in the battles he could face. Sometimes there could be a surprise attack as he traveled along, but the well thought out design of this shield kept him from danger in any circumstance.

The shield was made of wood and animal skin. The wood was covered by six layers of skin that had been meticulously treated and sewn together. The treated leather made the wooden shield very strong and if cared for accurately, it was literally impenetrable.

We have to take every measure to make our shields as impenetrable as that of the soldier. Any area of our shield that becomes dry and brittle will leave room for our foe to sneak in one of his vile arrows. They are fiery, deadly and are meant to kill. Jesus said in John 10:10 that, *"The thief comes only to steal and kill and destroy; ...."*

This thief that Jesus describes is none other than that serpent of old. He's still telling lies and being his manipulative, conniving self just as he was in the garden, where he deceived our original parents.

Ladies, it's very important to understand that we cannot overtake this powerful rival. He's too cunning, smooth and astute for us to match wits with. But your Champion, Lion of Judah, Sword carrying Warrior, Jesus can. He has defeated the Devil and his cohorts. The Lord gave us this precious armor to protect us.

Chapter Thirteen

Brace Yourself!

So then faith cometh by hearing, and hearing by the word of God. (Romans 10:17 KJV)

Jesus knows Satan extremely well. He created him from the beginning of time. He was beautiful and was in the very presence of God but evil was found in him. The Devil tried to usurp God's throne unsuccessfully and was thrown out of the presence of God and out of Heaven.

Jesus knows what is in him—evil, darkness and a wicked desire to destroy man to get back at God. He wants to be God, so he will stop at nothing to create his own kingdom—his followers, those who live without God, those who say, there is no God. They themselves become their own gods.

We, however, are the children of God. We have been saved by Jesus Christ and His unselfish sacrifice on the cross. We have been given this arsenal that is mighty and powerful. This shield we have is even more impenetrable than that of a mortal soldier.

In the morning, when the warrior woke, he had a schedule given to him that was adhered to by all the troops. How to care for his shield was at the top of that list. The soldier's life depended on the care of his shield. So how was this weapon kept in top shape? Every day the first thing he did was to take up his shield, take a little cup of heavy oil and would begin to carefully rub it—making sure not one inch was left unoiled.

My Friend, this is also the case for Christians. We need to care for our shields even more than we care for our hair, our nails and our own bodies. Just as we care about our skins and the softness and suppleness of it, so we need to care for our heavenly shield.

Our shield needs a good daily dose of oil, a smearing that will keep its suppleness and sturdiness. But how do I do that? you say. Every day our faith needs to be fed and re-enforced since this is an area that Satan looks to weaken. A shield that is dry and without the right amount of protection is susceptible to fiery darts that will destroy our shield of faith and leave us unprotected.

So, what are those fiery darts anyway? Well, for some it could be hatred, anger and rage. A childhood experience that has been engraved in our minds and hearts can be a deadly, fiery dart. It could be a struggle with self-esteem. These arrows, soaked with the poison of unforgiveness, will surely be extremely detrimental to our spiritual well-being. So, how do we guard ourselves from the onslaught of negativity, fear and doubt?

Satan knows exactly where we are in that area of our faith. When I say our faith, I don't mean our church affiliation, I mean the way we flex our Godly muscles and let him know how strong we are in our trust in Jesus. The Bible teaches us that Hebrews 11:1 that,

"Now faith is the substance of things hoped for, the evidence of things not seen." (Hebrews 11:1 KJV)

Jesus is our warrior King; He is the Lion of Judah. He is feared by Satan and He will keep us safe if we take care to water and oil our shield of faith. We must know without any doubt what the Word has to say about us and who we are and about this war we're in. Our recipe for success is within its beautiful pages.

When the troops went to war, they did something very interesting. They took their shields and put them in a trough like basin and soaked them for a day or so. The idea was for it to be completely wet so that when the enemy's fiery arrows hit his shield, they would be extinguished, put out. Wow! Talk about a method that works, no way to set that shield on fire that has been soaked in His Word and moving forward in faith.

What of our shields? How do we ready them for the battle before us? Well girls, just as you take care to hydrate your bodies, you need to hydrate your weapon as well. We set about with our fancy water bottles and are careful to measure our daily intake. For me, its very important because I tend to dehydrate so quickly. My water bottle (it's all blinged out of course) is my companion, because I know what will happen if my cells are not properly cared for.

Spiritually speaking friends, I know that I need to take time to keep my faith strong, unmovable and to let my enemy know that I mean business. His weapon, his fiery darts are not going to bring me down because I have soaked my soul in the water of the Word. This soaking makes me strong, courageous and I become a deadly weapon against the Devil in God's hands. The battle is mine. Jesus handed that down to all believers, but if I don't know what He says about my power and strength in Him, then I will lose.

Paul says in Romans 8:37 "...we are more than conquerors through Him that love us." That is so amazing, more than any general or any other human conqueror, you are more than that. Let's charge on girls! You have what it takes!

Chapter Fourteen

Oiled and Ready to Go!

"... The LORD's word is flawless; he shields all who take refuge in him." (2 Samuel 22:31)

How beautiful to know that God shields us from harm! He becomes our complete covering from the heat of battle. When we are facing temptations and just the hardships of life, the Lord is already there. His strong arm is always ready to fight for us.

In the verse above, it says that His Word is flawless. Isn't that awesome? I mean, just think about it, we can count on the fact that there is no error in it. I don't know about you, but I can't say that about anything I say or do. Flawless!

We can take refuge in knowing that He is forever Faithful, Trustworthy, a Protector for all who love Him. We never have to worry about the Presence of God in our souls if we take care to keep that open communication with Him on a daily and regular basis.

We can't just whip out our cracked shields and expect

them to protect us from the oncoming shower of fiery arrows. And let me tell you Ladies, and I'm sure you can relate, this aggressive strike from the Enemy can be very devastating. It can mean the end for some.

The importance of keeping our shields oiled with the Spirit of God and watered in His Word is the most valuable thing in our lives. We can't possibly face the difficult days that will surface in our time in this world unless we have taken care of this most essential weapon.

I'm not a morning person. I do mornings only when necessary or if someone decides for me that it is necessary. You know, like your kids or girlfriends who decide to call you before your eyelids have separated.

When I finally get up to greet my day, the first one I want to talk to is my Lord. I need to be alert and remember that I am still in this life. Sometimes, I have to think about that especially when I sense that peace and love. I can almost hear angels singing!

But I get a dose of reality when I hear a phone ring or a doorbell that calls me frantically to open the door. Distractions like this can take away our desire to focus on the Word. We had every intention and were determined to talk to Jesus first thing; before the world was up!

I understand! This is more the norm in our busy lives than the exception. It's like things are just waiting to happen the minute you wake up. My sisters, I get it, we just can't seem to do that one thing that is so important to us. Just a little time with Jesus, please!

But here's the thing, even though your desire is pure, the enemy is just waiting in the sidelines, salivating and waiting for just the right arrow to fling at you. Yep! You guessed it, guilt. "How can you say you love God when you can't even find time for Him? What kind of a Christian are you?" Blah, blah, blah!

Those are the words most of us hear when the Devil has been the one to create those distractions for us. Now he wants us to feel less than what Jesus says we are; beautiful, redeemed, accepted and forgiven. This how our Heavenly Father wants us to feel. He does not lay a guilt trip on us because we didn't drop to our knees the minute we woke up. Our Father, our Daddy God, waits for us.

I don't know what each morning will bring, (who does) but I am purposed in my heart that even though my commitment to spend time with the Holy Spirit first thing will not always happen, that as soon as I am able, I will do it.

Nothing can stop me from talking to the Lord, I do it as soon as I wake. I may not have the time to spend that special, prayer closet time with Him yet, but I will speak to Him in my heart as I go about my day. That prayer always includes, *"Lord, please help me find that little bit of time with just You."* He does, I go about the day excited to find Him in a moment in my car, no noise, just the two of us. It could be while I do laundry or wash dishes. (I know it sounds strange, but I love to wash dishes. I find it very spiritual)

There are many opportunities during the day, dear

sisters, where you can talk to your Lord. We have allowed others to decide for us what our prayer time and communication with God should be. Books have been written about the correct posture and time we need to spend with God in order to have a good prayer life.

For one thing, Jesus told us to be brief, not as the pagans who went on and on to impress others. Not to say that we should pray, "hello God" amen. It's our hearts that God sees and cares about. He knows your intentions and He sees your desire for Him. Trust me, if this is the case, He will make sure to make that time for the two of you.

The water of His Word; how wonderful it is to soak in it. There's just nothing like it. No matter what we may be feeling when we open it, by the time we're done, our hearts are light. We find courage and inspiration within its pages.

Immersing ourselves in the pages of the Scriptures is like drinking a refreshing cup water of water when we are parched.

Our souls get parched and dry, they call out from their depth for water. I love what Psalm 42: 1-2 says about thirst;

[1] *"As the deer pants for the water brooks, so pants my soul for You, O God.* [2] *My soul thirsts for God, for the living God."*

Isn't that so beautiful? Can you feel yourself panting for the Presence of God, longing to hear His voice in the pages of Scripture? I am feeling that need right now as I talk to you about it. So my Friends, let's oil up those shields, dunk them in the waterfalls of the Bible and get ready to ward off every flaming dart that may come against your soul.

These are uncertain times we live in. Our world is coming apart. It is changing and abounding in sin as Jesus said in Matthew 24. There's no stopping it, but you don't have to fall prey to any of it. You just keep that shield oiled and watered and march on valiantly.

It's impossible to memorize the entire Bible, but we can try to learn some verses to keep tucked away in our heart's treasure box. The more we read it, the more the Holy Spirit can bring to recollection during our times of battle. No matter what the need may be, He is able to give you that "now" Word. The one you need for that very specific moment.

Technology has made it possible for us to have the Word at our fingertips all the time. Our phones seem to be almost surgically affixed to us. We even sleep with them close by. Let us be as diligent with God's Word.

We have the ability to open that Bible app and go straight to His Word. You could be shopping and waiting to pay, pull out your virtual Word and read. How about while you're waiting in a doctor's office or for your child's school bus? These are just a few suggestions on how you can stay watered in His Word. As I mentioned earlier in another chapter, just the same way we are careful to carry those water bottles, we can be careful and diligent to carry that Bible with us.

Bible apps offer different studies you can engage in. They have devotionals that really only take a few minutes. Perhaps you can do one while you are waiting. Try it!

So, dear ones, there are many things that keep us from that special time we want to spend with Jesus, but there are just as many other things that help us to avail ourselves of His Word and to be ever so close to His Spirit, the Oil!

I know that we are pulled in many directions during our day, we are mothers and sisters and have families and jobs that require our attention. It's not easy to give our total being to anyone, right? But we must. I don't mean that you will be on your knees 24/7. That's not what the Apostle Paul meant when he said to pray without ceasing. What I mean is that you will have Jesus so close to you that you will not want to lose one single thought regarding Him.

My desire for you is that you are in love with Jesus and that the very thought of Him inundates your soul with love, peace and hope!

Section Five

The Helmet of Salvation

Chapter Fifteen

The Battlefield

"For our struggle is not against flesh and blood..."
(Ephesians 6:12)

Have you ever sat down to talk with God and suddenly you have a barrage of thoughts rushing in? Your mind becomes cluttered with the friend you forgot to call, the chores you didn't complete, the bill you forgot to pay, the kids' soccer schedules —your mind is now cluttered and unable to concentrate on God, the reason you went off by yourself to begin with.

Inevitably there is a struggle to keep our minds focused on the Lord. We struggle to retain His Word in our hearts and it seems we can't remember the powerful verses we've memorized for those particular occasions when Satan pushes against the tide of our minds. In Ephesians 6:12, the verse above, Paul tells us that this battle, our fight, is not against other people, but against an evil doer who wants to trespass God's territory in our hearts and destroy us.

Satan enters the battlefield through our senses and takes possession of our minds and thoughts if we let him.

We are going to look at the ways through which the enemy of our souls comes in. His ambition is to conquer our souls. Jesus called Satan a liar from the beginning of the world.

"...He was a murderer from the beginning, not holding to the truth, for there is no truth in him. When he lies, he speaks his native language, for he is a liar and the father of lies." (John 8:44)

He's still a liar! His goal and aim is to get us to buy into the lies he throws at us. He is an opportunist as we learn from Jesus' dealing with him in the desert during His forty days of fasting. That portion of Scripture tells us that Satan left Him for a more opportune time. (*The Cross*) He looks for opportunities in our day to implant those vicious lies he tries to inject into our minds.

Believers have been given a spiritual helmet that protects us against the bombardment of thoughts that he desires to infuse into our thought life. He hates us and will stop at nothing, *and I mean nothing*, to destroy us.

We have to be on our guard so that we're not taken in by the Devil's lies. The Enemy baited two holy, perfect beings—Adam and Eve—who fell for Satan's mis-representation of what God had commanded. Satan questioned Eve, "did God really say that?" This was Lucifer's first attempt to deceive mankind—if he deceived them, who saw and spoke with God daily, what will he do to us who live in a fallen world?

The battlefield will always take place in our minds. It begins there but we don't have to be dupped by him. The Holy Spirit is very familiar with all Satan's schemes.

The Lord calls us through the Holy Spirit and warns of the imminent danger that is lurking. If we walk with the Spirit, then we will not be taken in.

The helmet of Salvation offers us complete protection from our enemy's treacherous schemes. Salvation through Christ did more than cleanse us from all our sins. It provides full protection for the Believer.

The more we know about God's protection, the more victorious we will be in this age-old battle launched by Satan in the garden against man.

I pray you come out an even more equipped soldier at the end of this section. So, let's go!

Chapter Sixteen

Protection Guaranteed

"He only is my rock and my salvation; he is my defense; I shall not be greatly moved." (Psalm 62:2 KJV)

In this chapter we will consider three ways in which the enemy tries to gain control over our thought life. He is a conniving deceiver and is powerful. But we have an all-powerful Lord who fought the war and won.

We will discuss the spiritual mind and how having vs. not having our helmets on will affect each and every one of us. It will reveal how we see God, the World and the Devil.

I pray and hope that you will see why it's so important for us to have our helmets securely on.

The Eyes

The eyes are one of the gates that Satan wants to attack us through. We are visual people, so the eyes are the fastest way that sin can come into our minds. The things we see and lust after money, position, possessions could take root in our minds and destroy us from within.

We have a constant barrage from the media luring us into its murky net of lustful desires. We see beautiful things and we chase after them without considering the consequences. We go into debt only to have them make us prisoners of our weaknesses. But the Lord has given His children the protection we need to overcome the lust of the eyes.

Our eyes can be a cause to sin and separate us from the Lord or, they can become God's eyes on the earth. We can see what is wrong and set out to right it. We can see the needs and pain of others and minister to that.

Maintaining our spiritual eyesight is not easy in the world we live in, but it is possible. The Holy Spirit will come and help us fight that battle and He will certainly give us the victory Jesus promised us.

The Roman helmet had cutouts around the ears that not only gave the soldier protection. It also allowed him to hear his commander's orders and battle calls.

The Ears

Our heavenly helmet also gives us the ability to hear our Commander's beckoning. This helmet comes equipped with obedience and surrender to the One who leads us in battle. Jesus is the One who won the war against Satan and all his power over us. Jesus said,

"My sheep listen to My voice..." *(John 10:27)*

A believer who has put on the helmet of salvation is conditioned to listen and to respond to the Lord's voice. We instinctively go in His direction not ours.

Satan wants to penetrate through that protection and whisper his deceitful lies into our thoughts. He needs very little room, he just wants a way in. Once he is in our thoughts, we have been defeated. We need to call on the One (Jesus) who can give us the victory.

The Devil wants to bring guilt over the past. He wants to bring confusion and unforgiveness to our hearts. His great plan is to get our ear and forge ahead with the constant throwing of lies he wants us to hear.

If our helmet is secure, we will hear the quiet voice of Jesus calling to us. He calls us by name and woos us back to the pasture. He is aware of the wolf, the destroyer but, as the Good Shepherd, He is there to protect us. What a wonderful Savior!

The Mouth

"The tongue has the power of life and death, and those who love it will eat its fruit." (Proverbs 18:21)

This verse is both an encouraging and discouraging proverb. It is as true today as it was when Solomon wrote it. It has the promise of life when the right words are spoken, but it also has a warning to those who live without caution to the words that come out of our mouths.

The tongue is perhaps the most damaging organ in our body. The bible speaks of the tongue 500 times making this an important topic. James said in chapter 3,

"... but no human being can tame the tongue. It is a restless evil, full of deadly poison." (James 3:8)

I think we can all relate to that. I believe this is a very difficult area for women. The tongue is a far more difficult to control. We are emotional creatures and we can be quick to say things that are hurtful. We allow ourselves to get caught up in the emotion of the moment.

We can be critical of others. We pass on judgment all too quickly when we are angry and say words that have venom on the tip of our tongue. The enemy is always available to supply the poison. He has a great desire to hurt you and the one you speak against. Kill two minds with one poisoned dart.

The only way that we can avoid eating the bad fruit of our words is to give our mouths to the Lord. Our mouths were made to praise Him. It is in praise that we are able to

Our hearts are a well. It is either full of good or bad water. The well cannot have two types of water. The key to taming our tongues is to make sure that the well of our hearts is filled with the Word of God and that the One who stirs that water is the Spirit of God. We need to have the willingness to hear His voice and obey it.

Jesus said, *"...for the mouth speaks what the heart is full of." (Luke 6:45)*

The Lord had much to say about our words. Our words mean a great deal to Him. If we are His children, then goodness, humility and gentleness must be found in us. We are His heart, His words here on earth.

An unhealed heart can be a deadly weapon when it has not allowed the Holy Spirit to heal its wounds. Traumatic experiences and hurts can claim our thoughts, emotions and actions when not kept in check.

Numerous studies have shown that traumas and tragedies are engraved in our brains and stored in our sub-conscience minds and when triggered, our moods and behaviors can change and making us vulnerable for sin.

What an amazing brain! What an incredible and intelligent, creative God! He thought of everything. He knew that sin which produces tragedies in the lives of His children would leave indelible marks on our hearts.

Jesus equipped us with the right protection, the helmet of salvation, so that we could fend off those pesky memories that wreak havoc with our hearts and minds.

The Roman soldier tied his helmet firmly, to the point of creating a callous under his chin. We too need to have our helmet of salvation firmly on with calloused chins. We have to stand against the lies that Satan hurls at us regarding our salvation. Let us hurl back his accusations and let him know that

"whosoever believeth on Him will be saved." (John 3:16)

Put your helmet on tight and firm dear sister, let us join forces and advance towards the gates of the enemy with confidence and truth. ***You, are a Warrior Princess!***

Chapter Seventeen

One Size Fits All

"If we confess our sins, he is faithful and just to forgive us our sins and to cleanse us from all unrighteousness." (1John 1:9)

Our helmet of salvation is truly a "one size fits all." There is only one style and one size. We cannot pick and choose because it was designed to fit each and every believer perfectly. It provides protection for the entire head—our minds.

It was designed by our Commander in Chief Himself, Jesus, so that if worn properly, it would protect our minds and our souls. Jesus wants what is going on inside to be noticeable on the outside just like the adorning plumage of the Roman soldier.

The Helmet of Salvation brings numerous benefits and protection to the believer. It protects us from dangers and harm that we cannot see, hear or touch. These dangers are spiritual and can only be fought on a supernatural front. Paul says,

"Furthermore, just as they did not think it worthwhile to retain the knowledge of God, so God gave them over to a depraved mind, so that they do what ought not to be done." (Romans 1:18)

One of the great protections of the helmet is that our minds are kept for God. It saves us from a depraved mind. The mind that says there is no God; the mind that says I don't really have to obey God. I don't need God.

We no longer do as we did before but we are now wholly His. Unlike the depraved mind that comes to a person without God, to the Believer, salvation brings a mind renewal. Paul tells says,

> "Do not conform to the pattern of this world, but be transformed by the renewing of your mind..." (Romans 12:2)

A transformed mind no longer lives without hope, but it trusts in God and the plans that the Lord has for one's life.

> 'For I know the plans I have for you," declares the LORD, "plans to prosper you and not to harm you, plans to give you hope and a future. (Jeremiah 29:11)

Just as the Roman soldier's helmet protected him from surprise attacks, we too are kept from Satan's oncoming surprise blows. God Himself is our rear guard.

> "...the LORD will go before you, the God of Israel will be your rear guard." (Isaiah 52:12)

We have protection against spiritual death and the vile evil that our enemy wants to inject into our minds. If Satan can rob us of the healthy and pure mind that Christ has given us through salvation, then he can take away our peace and our joy. We would be constantly wondering if God is still there in every situation we face.

We would be on our guards, looking over our shoulders hoping that the Lord hasn't forgotten us.

The helmet of salvation covers our minds against the enemy's fiery darts. It protects us from becoming renegades against God and from crippling fear. Attacks will come, but the Lord has reassured us of His eternal and healing love. We throw off fear.

"For God hath not given us the spirit of fear; but of power, and of love, and of a sound mind." (2 Timothy 1:7 KJV)

Satan comes at us with mindsets and attitudes that are deadly. I am talking about those days when you don't even want to get out of bed, when your day isn't going as planned!

You know what I'm talking about¾when things are so bad, whether real or perceived, that you just want to pull the blanket over your head and never wake up. I can honestly tell you that I have had and still have more of those days than I care to talk about.

The enemy wants to penetrate our minds through the three gates whereby he can bring sin into our lives.

The Roman helmet protected the eyes, the ears and the mouth. Just as the roman soldier was protected in these areas by his helmet, so are we by the helmet of salvation.

Our helmet transforms us. Romans 12:2 sways that we are not to be transformed by the world and its idea of what we should think or be but that we are to be transformed by the renewing of our minds. One bad thought in, take it out and replace it with God's Holy

Word. This will certainly transform, change and bring peace to the way we think and feel about ourselves. We are to bring every thought captive under Christ's submission and authority.

> "*We demolish arguments and every pretension that sets itself up against the knowledge of God, and we take captive every thought to make it obedient to Christ" (2 Corinthians 10:5 NIV)*

We can turn our eyes away and think on those things that Paul said,

> "*...Finally, brothers and sisters, whatever is true, whatever is noble, whatever is right, whatever is pure, whatever is lovely, whatever is admirable, if anything is excellent or praiseworthy—think about such things." (Philippians 4:8)*

Chapter Eighteen

Putting on The Helmet

"...take the helmet of salvation." (Ephesians 6: 17)

I love fashion! One thing I have a fascination for is hats. I love, love the many choices! I have a good selection of them and I love them all.

Since the first thing we do is shower, we can start here. Before putting on our best, we want to be clean. Jesus bathed us in His blood so that we would be *white as the snow;* salvation, *His best.*

The next thing we do after bathing is to put on our garment onto which we put on the belt as we discussed in the previous section of this book, but the helmet is the protection for our heads. After bathing we love to fix our hair. We fuss with it and work it until we are pleased with it. Unless you are like me with my short spiky hair and you just rub your head and go. (*I hear that hiss.*) I know! You're envious!

The hair is our crowning glory. It is meant to be a covering for our heads, a protection from some injuries and those pesky bugs. We could have the most beautiful outfit on but if our hair is not cooperating it could ruin our entire day.

I feel that if I am fitted with my helmet before anything else, that all the other parts come much easier. The helmet covers all the vital parts of the head. It protects the ears, the eyes and the mouth; the portals through which sin enters a person.

The Roman soldier's helmet was strategically made. It had a slope in the rear part to protect him from a surprise attack and prevent him from loosing his head.

I realize that I am dating myself here but this curvy part of the helmet reminds me of one of those big hairdos we wore back in the 70s called a "flip." Who came up with these names? Imagine, calling a hairdo a flip during a time when we were "flipping out."

The Roman soldier's helmet was one of the most important parts of his gear. It was originally made from leather that went through a hardening process of tanning.

From the second century BC and into the first century AD the Romans began to make their helmets out of thin sheets of metals such as steel, bronze and copper.

These helmets were beautifully crafted and were sometimes adorned with gold especially those of the commanding officers. Soldiers of lower ranks would use brass instead of gold in the areas of the helmet that they wanted to stand out.

The tops of the helmets had plumes that identified the soldier's rank. Only high-ranking soldiers wore plumes. The plumes were made of horse hair and dyed in different colors such as red, black or white.

The soldier wore it like a badge of honor and how it was displayed had to do with his rank. The Commander of a group of soldiers wore his plume from front to back and it was both a sign of rank and also a way of showing their position in battle so that the men could identify with their leader. During heated battle they would look to see if their leader was still alive and engaged in the fight.

The Centurion was a leader under the Commander. He had one hundred men in his charge and wore his plumage from side to side to show his rank. In the same way the Centurion looked to his Commander, his men would look to his plumage which made him stand taller than the soldiers. As long as they could see the plumage of their leader, they were encouraged to continue fighting.

The helmet was a defensive weapon and was designed with the soldier's protection in mind. It was made to protect the soldier's entire head from harm. An unprotected head could mean sure death. It had cutouts around the ears so that not only did the soldier have protection, but he could also hear his commander's orders.

In order to protect the jaws and mouth, it had flaps that wrapped around the cheeks ending at the mouth. It would be disastrous for a soldier to receive an unprotected blow to the cheeks. The soldier would not be able to speak and call out for help. This would not only put him in danger but could also put his comrades at risk.

Additionally, he would not be able to sustain himself and might die because he would not be able to eat or drink. The death of a soldier not only affected the morale of the entire unit, but their numbers were affected as well.

A rim at the top front protected the forehead so a sword was averted before it could do any serious damage. The soldier's attention and importance to the helmet was such that it was laced so tightly that he had a sore under his chin. It was crucial that this part of the gear did not come loose while the soldier was in battle. A loose helmet would mean certain death.

It is imperative for the Believer to have their helmets on firmly and secure. Salvation is not something we've done but it's what Christ has accomplished on the cross. It is crucial that we understand this, we will perish if we don't invite Jesus into our lives without reserve. We cannot serve Him halfhearted, but with passion and commitment that He deserves.

When we live by the truth that "we are His and He is ours", then we can live secure in Jesus' protection, and be always affirmed in the truth "that nothing can snatch us away from His hand." When Satan attacks our minds, we must check our helmet's stability and ask ourselves; Am I standing on the truths Jesus taught us in His Gospel.

Allowing the Devil to question our salvation is taking a blow that can damage our soul needlessly. We need stand firm and have the Helmet of Our Salvation on tight, just as the Roman soldier knew how important that protection was, so we must give it even greater importance. Let's stay in this fight together!

Section Six

The Sword of The Spirit

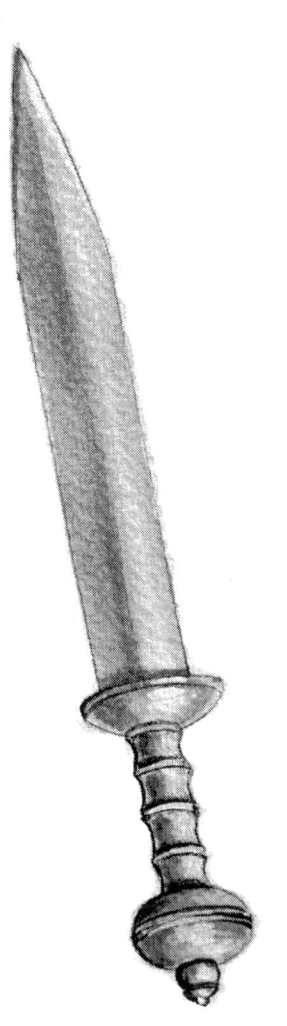

Chapter Nineteen

Two Sides to Everything

"...take up the... sword of the Spirit, which is the word of God." (Ephesians 6:17)

One of the most amazing defensive weapons we have is the Sword of the Spirit—the Word of God. No weapon was more evident in Jesus' ministry than that of the Sword of the Spirit.

In Matthew's account of the temptation of Christ, we learn that the Devil didn't stop at one try, he went all out.

Matthew 4:1-10 records this account. It says that Jesus was led into the desert by the Holy Spirit to be tempted by Satan. There, He fasted for 40 days and nights. At the end of His fast, when His body was weak and He was in much need of food, water and rest, Satan came to tempt Him.

In the first temptation, Satan tries to take advantage of the Lord's physical weakness by offering Him bread. He was quick to pounce on the opportunity when Jesus was fatigued and hungry. He thought for sure that the Lord would cave into his offering of bread. But Jesus responds with the Sword of God's Word.

> ... *"It is written: 'Man shall not live on bread alone, but by every word that comes from the mouth of God." (Matthew 4:4)*

What a wallop! I'm sure Satan didn't see that coming. Hopefully, we have learned from past experiences that he doesn't give up so easily. If one thing doesn't work, he'll try something else.

In The second temptation, Satan takes Him to the highest place at the holy city, the pinnacle of the Temple, by saying, "if you are the Son of God then throw yourself down. For it is written that He will command His angels to take charge of you."

> *Jesus answered him, "It is also written: 'Do not put the Lord your God to the test." (Psalm 91)*

The audacity of him to try to entice the Lord with a question that was meant to create doubt. It was an *I dare you*. But Jesus did not respond to that because He knew who He was. He was the only Son of God.

Satan's goal was to get Jesus to test God by throwing Himself off the temple's highest peak. He was seeking Jesus' premature death and therefore there would be no cross by which we could be saved. Clever right? But God always foils his dastardly efforts.

Satan knows the Scriptures more expertly than any theologian or biblical scholar that ever was. He can quote it accurately but his aim is always to deceive and confuse.

He is quick to quote Psalm 91 which says that "... He will send His angels concerning you." But I love the Lord's response, again another big blow to him when Jesus responds:

> "It is also written: 'Do not put the Lord your God to the test.'" (Matthew 4:7)

How well the enemy knows how to voice the Word of God, he uses it very conveniently. The problem is that he likes to twist it just so. He desires to bend God's truth and get us to believe something other than what the Lord has said or means. He is a lying conniver. He wants to get into our minds as he did with Eve, by first asking "did God really say that?" or as we see in Matthew's account, by getting Jesus to question who He was, and he does with us.

In the third temptation, the Tempter comes to Jesus once again. On this occasion, while Jesus is still in the desert after his fast, he takes the Lord to a very high mountain and shows Him all the kingdoms of the world and all their riches and splendor if He will just worship him. The Lord's response;

> "Away from me, Satan! For it is written: 'Worship the Lord your God, and serve Him only.'" (Matthew 4:10)

In each one of these situations Jesus' response is the Word of God, "it is written," and BAM, a sharp sword that pierced through Satan's core. By the third time it says that Satan left him for a more well-planned time. Will he come back? Absolutely! He came to Jesus once again during His agony and resurrection.

The Word of God is our most effective weapon. It is carried by the Holy Spirit to our souls and minds so that we can fight the good fight. When we are in a battle against temptation, our foe's intention is to get us to fall back to our old ways; lying, gossip, immorality and the sinful thoughts and the such that clutter our minds and keep us from meditating on God's life giving Word.

"I meditate on your precepts and consider your ways." (Psalm 119:15)

What a powerful statement. It's plain to see how much David loved the Lord and His Word. I desire to be like David; to meditate always on His Word and obey it! If we can reflect and be intentional about being a doer of the Word and not just a hearer, then we can live up to the words spoken by Paul, "we are more than conquerors in Christ Jesus." And we are!

Chapter Twenty

Hand to Hand Combat

"Fight the good fight..." (I Timothy 6:12)

The Roman troops preferred a sword known as the "gladius," which is the Latin word for a sword with two edges. The word is correctly translated "two mouths" in the Hebrew. We read in the Bible that God's Word is a two-edged sword or a two-mouthed sword.

This gladius was the only offensive weapon in their entire gear. Measuring from 18" to 21", it was easy to handle and perfect for up close and personal fighting. It was also widely used by the gladiators in the fight to the death combats in the Roman arenas.

The gladius was the sword used by the Romans for over 400 years and was the weapon that helped them conquer most of the known world. The troops hung their sword on

their belts in the scabbard which was on the left or right side for quick and easy access.

Our sword is the Word of God, anointed by the Holy Spirit. It hangs on the belt of truth. It is our faith in that Word and the veracity of it that allows it to become a powerful weapon.

When we believe that the words in the Bible come from the very mouth of God, we speak them in faith because we believe in the One who spoke the Word. We speak those words because we believe they have the power to accomplish that which God said they would and it would not return to Him without hitting the target.

When we are being tempted, we wield the mighty sword of the Word of God. The words we speak have the power to kill or to bring life. It is for this reason that we need to pray God's Word.

I have prayed God's Word during many hard times in my life such as illness. I have prayed this prayer:

"Lord, I thank you because your Word is Faithful. You are the God of truth on which I hang my faith. You are for me and not against me. You are my present help in time of trouble. Your word says that all my infirmities were nailed to the cross on Calvary. By your stripes I am healed. Lord, I thank you for my healing. Your Word is truth and I believe in every word that comes from the mouth of my God. Though I faint to the point of death, I know that the same Spirit that raised Christ from the dead will raise my mortal body, this body that I now have."

Is this a prayer that God can work with? You bet your high heels He can! They are the words that came out of the Bible.

The Roman soldier used his sword to wound his enemy quickly and effectively. The wound was quick and deep and was meant to kill instantly.

Christians have a short, swift sword as well. God's Word does not have to be the "sermon on the mount," girls. Jesus taught us to be brief, not to be like the pagans with their smart, intellectual words that were meant to impress. Prayer is talking to God from our hearts.

When Jesus was in the boat and the storm arose, He commanded the elements and simply said, "be still," nothing more. When He went to Jairus' house, He told the little girl to wake up and she did. The Sword of His Word pierced death and the grave and they simply obeyed. The Scriptures hold the same power now as they did then and forever. They will never pass away.

How are you handling your temptations? Is your sword a two-edge sword like the Roman soldier's? Is it always sharp

with the practice and knowledge of the Word of God or is it dull because you never take it out? Do you wear it for show, or just to accessorize the rest of your outfit? Do you know when it's time to pull it out to purposely wound your enemy?

Our swords are mighty weapons, this sword, God's Word, is mighty for the binging down of strongholds (2 Corinthians 10:4). Many of us are defeated because we don't know what the Word of God has to say regarding our present circumstances so we are overtaken even though we had the best defense all along.

Our swords become rusty and unusable because they are not in constant use. We fly into enemy territory without protection. We want to fight and win but we have gone into battle in our underwear without our battle dress. The sword that God gave us is more powerful than any sword that Satan can wield or forge against you.

Chapter Twenty-One

Get a Grip

"I have fought the good fight; I have finished the race..." (2 Timothy 4:7 KJV)

One thing that a soldier must do is get a good, strong grip on his weapon. Whether in ancient times or with today's well trained fighting machines, the weapon must be firmly in hand. If the enemy makes aggressive contact with that weapon, one thing is for sure, the soldier will lose total control and perish in the fight. A police officer is trained to never give up his weapon because doing so will endanger him and perhaps another; he can become a hostage of the perpetrator.

I know I keep making reference to soldiers, but ladies, that is exactly what we are, we're soldiers. You and I are warriors in the Lord's great army of believers. Wow! I don't know about you, but I see myself wielding that sword about and letting the enemy know who's the boss—Jesus, of course!

The reason for the preferred short swords was because this allowed the infantrymen to be very intentional about hitting the intended target. The gladius was about 18" to 24" in length and was light and very effective in combat. The opponent's swords were long and did not give them enough space to move around or get as close to the opponent. The motion was choppy and not as deadly as the gladius. The opponent's long sword was also one sided and didn't do nearly the damage that the two-edged gladius did.

Sometimes the swords we hold are not the right swords, they can be long and choppy and cutting nothing. We speak biblical words but without the power that only comes from the Holy Spirit and from a pure heart. Our intention is to get either God's attention in prayer or to rebuke the enemy. Our motives are not sincere.

In either case, we fail. We run around chopping away in the wind without any real target. We must have a target—Satan and all his dark and vile cohorts. We need to wield a sword that is dripping with the anointing and power of God's Holy Spirit.

When we have a plentiful number of Scriptures hidden in our hearts, and if securely placed on the belt of truth, our integrity of life, then that sword along with the truth of His Word comes alive in us. They then have an invincible power over the darkness and evil that tries to plunge us back into the life we came from before we surrendered our lives Christ.

The legionnaire could move with ease. He could duck and was able to attack his unsuccessful challenger. When we use God's Word as it is intended to be used, we too can move easily and with great agility leaving the forces of darkness ineffective against us. We will be able to do serious damage to the kingdom of darkness if we learn to use our trusty sword, the Word of the Spirit.

We can never loosen our grip—not even for a split second. The Roman soldier trained rigorously and practiced, practiced, practiced. Isn't that what Jesus' army should do as well? We can never put down our Sword but it should be used daily and, as I mentioned earlier, there is great power when we pray the Word of God in every circumstance.

There is an old adage that says, "practice makes perfect." Paul says in Hebrews 10:14, *"For by one sacrifice he has made perfect forever those who are being made holy."*

So, we continue in the fight using our faithful Sword daily, constantly, as we become stronger and stronger so that we can wage war against Satan empowered and invincible in our day of battle.

Chapter Twenty-Two

To The Hilt

"...He has made My mouth like a sharp sword..." (Isaiah 49:2 KJV)

Warfare was bloody and very vicious anywhere but most especially in the Roman Empire. The thought of them coming to a town near you put fear in the hearts of people. They left no witnesses; they would ferociously kill the entire village and all its inhabitants. You can understand why people trembled at the thought of this army coming to their town.

Earlier we talked about the gladius and the powerful, effective weapon that it was. Even though all that was needed was a 3" to 4" penetration, the soldier would plunge his sword right through to the hilt. The hilt was the metal part of the sword that went all the way to the top, just before the handle. It was very important to have a firm grip so that the hand would not slide down the sword and injure the fighter.

Can you imagine yourself doing the same to Satan and his kingdom? When we live with integrity and hold God's precepts in our hearts, we can deliver a deep, devastating blow to our adversary. We thrust our swords to the hilt.

Jesus had no mercy on the Devil; he quoted the Scriptures when Satan tried to tempt Him. This is a perfect example of driving in that sword right to the end. That day, the Lord ripped Satan apart to the point that he had to depart. He cannot stand truth and especially the sound of God's Word being spoken.

When we thrust the Sword backed up with a life of integrity and with the knowledge of the Scriptures which are hidden in our hearts, then the blow to our oppressor will be devastating. When I'm being tempted to sin against God, I have a heart full of His Word and it tells me that I am His prized possession, I am His and He is mine. It reminds me that He will never leave me nor forsake me. God is never too busy to be my Warrior, the One who fights my battles.

Sometimes life can feel like nothing is going to change. Every day, every month, every year we seem to battle against the same thing. We play our defeats over and over in our minds like a movie and we forget the many victories we've had through the Sword of the Spirit.

I love what Jeremiah says in chapter 20:11

"But the LORD is with me like a fearsome warrior. Therefore, my persecutors will stumble and will not prevail."

The Lord brings dread to the kingdom of darkness. Imagine when He showed up after His death, the enemy was defeated forever.

I mentioned earlier about the dread and fear that befell people when they heard the Romans were coming. But imagine the fear that the opponent of our souls feels when He sees God coming to our rescue. No wonder he fled in the desert when He tried to tempt the Lord. When it comes to battling God, the Devil is a cowardly opponent and a bully.. He doesn't stand a chance.

Jesus is your fearless champion; He will stop at nothing to protect you from the harm of the battle against your eternal soul. Dear friend, there is nothing He won't do for you. The Lord understands our fears and our despair. When we just want to give up, He comes to our defense. King David called Him his hiding place. My sisters, its okay to hide as long as we are hiding in the Mighty Jehovah.

Psalm 91 is my favorite Psalm. I love how it starts:

[1] "He who dwells in the secret place of the Most High Shall abide under the shadow of the Almighty. [2]... He is my refuge and my fortress; My God, in Him I will trust."

What beautiful imagery of our God, He is always close and personal and forever available to His children—He is available to you. Jesus said that He would not leave us as orphans but that He would send us His Spirit to guide, to counsel and be the Guarantor of our Salvation. How amazing is that, Ladies? Talk about personal, He cared for us even as He awaited His death, He was already giving comfort to those He loved.

Therefore, we must keep those words in our hearts and allow them to comfort us, to change us. They were not mere words; they were power and life giving, life changing. Jesus' Spirit is still with us, His Words have the same power that they did when He created the world; they have not diminished with time but are as powerful and available to us to render the Enemy powerless against us.

So, Ladies, pick up that Sword! Let's march forward against that deceitful foe that wants to bring death and devastation to God's people. Are we to allow him to take our weapons rendering us useless? In no way! So I invite you to march forward with me, girls. Let's thrust our Swords to the hilt against that evil trespasser!

Chapter Twenty-Three

Use It or Lose It

"Keep this Book of the Law always on your lips; meditate on it day and night, so that you may be careful to do everything written in it..." (Joshua 1:8)

Girls, can a woman have too many shoes? I say not! But shoes are meant to be worn on a regular basis. Let me tell you a not so funny story. Well, some of you may think it funny. Actually, as I retell it, it does sound funny.

Some years ago, I remember going to my (*well stocked*) shoe rack and reached for a pair of shoes I hadn't worn in a while. They were red and oh so comfortable. I was excited to have just the right shoes to wear with my new outfit.

You know what I mean, that just perfect match to your outfit. But much to my stunning, and I mean stunning surprise, when I took the shoes down, they were rigid and unusable. The leather had become stiff and brittle and they literally fell apart in my hands. Disappointment is an understatement! If I had made a practice of wearing them more often, they would not have come to such a sad end.

Once I saw what happened to those favorite shoes, I realized that my shoes perished for lack of care. It was important for me to care for and instead of locking them up in an unbreathable box. Why am I talking about unused shoes? Well, I know that shoes don't compare to swords, but the two need care and use.

One thing that the Roman legionnaire did was to care for his sword. The sword was perhaps his most important weapon. It was made of metal and what happens when you leave a metal tool or item out in the element? They rust and are no longer usable and restoring an overly rusted tool is next to impossible.

The soldiers were careful not to leave their swords out in the elements. When the battle was over, they washed their swords of all the bloody mess and oiled them to keep them from rusting. They would also sharpen them to keep those edges sharp. Their opponents didn't stand a chance.

What do you do with your sword when you've just come out of a fierce battle with demons? Perhaps, like me, you have fought illness or the loss of a loved one. Maybe you have been financially devastated or lost everything you had. It seems you've been out in the battlefield far too long. You finally have a breakthrough and you can just let your guard down.

Did I just say let your guard down? Oh no, we never want to do that! We can never let our guard down or lay down this important weapon. If we don't care for it, it will surely rust. You know, the Sword of the Spirit, which is the Word, can be like that. I don't mean to say that God's Word gets rusty, far be it from me to say such a thing. What I mean is that if we don't search and meditate on and seek to understand it, our souls abandon its power and use and it becomes, due to our heart condition, an ineffective weapon.

I can't neglect the advantage I have in not only knowing the Scriptures but also knowing when and how to use them. Remember I said that

practice makes perfect, and it does. When I meditate on God's commands, His Words of comfort and instruction, then I become a strong warrior; one that is to be feared by the evil forces that attack me. But if I lay my Bible on a shelf and don't endeavor to learn it so that I can hide it in my heart, then it will not have the power I need it to have. When properly care for, oiled and sharpened, the Spirit brings it alive in me.

Remember that Satan quoted Scripture to Jesus and might I add he was most accurate. He had the words but they had no power. Why, because only darkness and evil were found in him. He's an 'if at first you don't succeed, try, try again' opponent. He's relentless and never, never gives up.

Having the Sword of the Spirit constantly stirring our hearts and minds will keep us from being defeated. Our enemy is very powerful, manipulative and cunning. He has many tricks up his wicked sleeve. It is for this reason that we need to be at the ready, always. Never, never lay your Sword down. Satan doesn't.

Section Seven

The Seventh Weapon

"And pray in the Spirit on all occasions with all kinds of prayers and requests...."
(Ephesians 6:18)

Back to our soldier! You haven't forgotten him, have you? I want to tell you a little more about him before we part ways. The Roman legionaries carried a weapon called the pilum; this is the Latin word for spear or lance. It ranged anywhere from six to seven feet in length and had a very strong point on it that was about twenty-four inches in length and about a quarter inch in diameter.

I know, this is too much information, right? But I want to form a visual for you. I'm going somewhere with this, just hang in there, don't lose me now!

Successful spear or lance throwing was an art form in itself. Mr. soldier couldn't afford to miss, his life depended on it. The first thing they did once engaged in battle, was to throw their flaming arrows, the second in line was the spear.

The pilum could go pretty far if the throw was right. What do I mean by that? Well, it wasn't just pulling it back and throwing it hoping it would hit the target. It was more about strategy and a disciplined mind whose one thought was to hit its target.

When the soldier poised himself to throw his spear, he gave it all he had. Have you ever watched the discus throwers at the Olympic games, the momentum that they build to see that discus go as far out as possible is amazing!

The Romans practiced their spears or lances throwing just as they did with sword wielding. A soldier couldn't just go out on the day of battle and hope that he would just throw his spears and snap, the enemy's gone, it was practice, practice, practice.

If the soldier wanted his lance to go further, then he would weight it by slipping metal rings to the middle of the weapon. This weight would allow the spear to go a greater distance making sure that his weapon would travel right smack in the middle of the enemy's formation lines. Imagine soldiers lined up side by side with their pila (plural) descending on their rivals. What a sight!

I love the beginning verse! Why you ask? Well because it's something that we do together—not just as individuals but as a people. When we come together in prayer, we are just like those Roman forces united in battle and with one purpose — down with the enemy!

The seventh weapon is intercessory prayer! It's something we do for others and with others.

> *"They all joined together constantly in prayer..."*
> *(Acts 1:14)*

The early church was fervent in their prayer lives. They had a very good example from their leaders, the Apostles and those who followed the early Church Fathers. They prayed on all occasions and for all their needs and circumstances.

There was never any doubt in their hearts that the Lord wasn't listening and that they would get an answer.

If you do a search of the types of prayers that are in the Bible you will find several. Listed below are some of those prayers.

Prayer of Faith *(James 5:15)*

Prayer of Thanksgiving *(Philippians 4:6)*

Prayer of Agreement *(Matthew 18:19)*

Prayer of Intercession *(I Timothy 2:1)*

Prayer for Deliverance *(Psalm 69:14)*

Prayer of Binding and Losing *(Ephesians 6:18)*

I'm sure that a more intense search will yield many prayers for you to consider. It's okay to repeat someone's prayer if you feel they are of benefit to your soul—after all, we repeat the Psalms, and that's what they are. The most famously repeated prayer all over the world, is the Lord's Prayer; this prayer is recited at funerals, public church gatherings, weddings just to name a few.

So no matter how you choose to pray, the important thing is that your heart means what your mouth proclaims, that you are surrendered to the Holy Spirit and that you are above all things, sincere in your worship.

Even though some prayers like the Psalms and the Lord's prayer are repeated, we also have to take care not to repeat prayers and sayings that are offered up to other gods. Jesus taught us not to repeat the vane sayings of the gentiles. He said they were repetitious *(chanting)* and long.

Prayer is having a conversation with God. We should not rehearse them anymore than we rehearse a conversation with another person. God wants the humility of our hearts with all its simplicity and genuineness.

Have you heard a child pray? I love to hear my grandchildren pray, they say whatever is on their little hearts without flowery words or phrases to impress God—they are pure and sincere. It is no wonder that Jesus hears them, this is perhaps one of the reasons why He told us to be like children—He didn't mean to become a child but to have that same pure heart attitude a child has.

In the list of Bible prayers, I included previously, I left one specific prayer for last intentionally. Why? Because it goes along with this seventh weapon I've been describing to you. That prayer is that we are to pray in the Spirit.

*"And pray **in the Spirit** on all occasions with all kinds of prayers and requests. (Ephesians 6:18)*

So, my understanding is that we should always pray with the assistance of the Holy Spirit because we don't always know how to pray. He will lead and guide us and pray for us. Does that mean that He will mouth the words for us? Of course not, what it means is that He will inspire us and move within our hearts so that we can express ourselves according to our needs.

In the same way, the Spirit helps us in our weakness. We do not know what we ought to pray for, but the Spirit himself intercedes for us through wordless groans. (Romans 8:26)

Our mandate is to pray in the Spirit always and for everything. The part about praying in the Spirit is Paul's way of saying, put weight around that spear!

If our prayers are not prayed with the weight of the Holy Spirit, they won't go as far as we need them to. The Spirit takes those troubled hearts that are not able to express themselves fully and He will make sure that your Heavenly Father receives the exact message it's trying to convey. That spear has been sent off with all the weight and power it needs to reach its intended target.

The Lord knows our hearts and as Jesus said, He knows what we need before we even ask. He's already done it my Friend. So, put weight on that spear of yours, shoot it out and wait for its response. Never doubt for a minute, the answer is on its way!

The Beginning

This should be called the conclusion however because this war will rage on till the Day of the Lord and we are finally home with Him, I thought it was best to describe it as the beginning and not the end.

I am grateful that you have gone on this journey with me. I pray that at the conclusion of this book that you have a greater understanding of that magnificent suit of armor and the One who made it especially for you.

My prayer is that you will "put on the full armor of God," so that when the day of trouble comes you will be found standing and immovable.

So, hold the line Ladies, keep your position—don't allow the enemy to break through. Let's lock arms in prayer, encourage one another and be the very best you can be—not perfect but excellent! Stay vigilant—prayed up and always, always yearning in your hearts for His magnificent return. I can hardly wait!!!

About the Author

Emily Quintero-Spongberg is a licensed minister, author, Bible teacher and speaker. She has four children, seven grandchildren and six great grandchildren. She resides in Connecticut with her husband Tim.

Emily was born in Camuy, Puerto Rico. Her parents moved to Connecticut in 1955 where she has lived ever since.

She has loved books and art since early childhood and her dream was to write a book someday. Emily is fully bi-lingual in Spanish—one of her goals is to translate her books into Spanish.

Pastor Emily is a leader in women's ministries and teaches at Crossroads Bible institute at her church in East Hartford, Connecticut. She has a desire to teach biblical truths in a simple way so that they can be understood and applied to the daily life of the Believer—and to develop *fully devoted followers of Christ.*

Emily has attended Bible school for many years—she attended the Spanish American Bible Institute in New Haven, CT, Koinonia Bible Institute in Coeur d'Alene, ID and is currently working on a degree in Theology with a focus on Women's Issues.

Emily has been teaching since 1967 and has taught children, youth, married couples and as she puts it; she has been promoted to teach adults.

In 1997 Emily wrote a children's book *Hannibal and King*. And she plans to continue writing other books that address spiritual matters concerning women. She also wants to continue her Hannibal and the King series. Her next book in the series is Hannibal's Song.